Goddess Enchantme

Magic and Spells

Volume 1: *Goddesses of the Seasons*

Written and photographed
by Carrie Kirkpatrick

'Themis' written by
Gareth Medway

Dearest Liv

Goddess Bless!

Lots of love

Carrie x

Grave Distractions Publications
Nashville, Tennessee
www.gravedistractions.com

Cataloging-In-Publication Data
Goddess Enchantment Magic and Spells:
Volume 1 Goddesses of the Seasons
Kirkpatrick, Carrie
ISBN: 978-0-9829128-4-3
1. Non-Fiction 2. Religions 3. Pagan 4.Practices

Cover Art: Christine Moloney
To see more of Ms. Moloney's artwork please visit: www.myartisyours.co.uk

Edition bound in the USA and UK by Lightning Source
Electronic versions of this text are available. For more information visit: www.gravedistractions.com
For eBook users, the images of the Goddesses in your eBook edition may be used in these rituals. Simply place your eReader on your altar with the image showing and complete the ritual outlined in the text.

Acknowledgements

Kleo Fanthorpe: Stylist, and for all her help and assistance.
Cover Art: Christine Moloney.
Researchers: Seldiy Bate, Gareth Medway and Maria Malo.
Graphic Design: Lewis Webb.
Photographic post production: Darren Richardson and Prapatson Richardson.
Additional photography: Kleo Fanthorpe, Alan Rider, Christine Moloney, Chris Robinson, production stills for *Hecate Rising* by Lorna Unwin-Wright for Divine Productions.
Shutterstock photo Library.
Jon Randall.
Brian Kannard from Grave Distractions Publications.

Models: Jinji Garland, Gemma Bowen, Jane, Christine Moloney, Adam Pamment, Anya Hastwell, Kero Kaneko-James, Kleo Fanthorpe, Oephebia Stars, Maria Antoniou, Caroline Robertson, Avril Elms, Sally Asbury.
Cast of *Hecate Rising*: Michael Bingas, Laura Daligan, Meredith Lee, and Marcus Wolfson.
A special thanks to everyone in the community that donated their time, wisdom, and sage advice in the creation of this book.

Index

Why Goddesses?

G oddesses of the Seasons takes you through the Pagan Wheel of the Year, honouring the ancient festivals that mark the Equinoxes, the Solstices and the Fire Festivals. Goddesses from different pantheons have been brought together in celebration of the festivals and they are brought to life with magical photographs. The story of each Goddess is accompanied by spells and visualisations, which can enhance your spiritual development and aid you in feeling a connection with the Goddesses.

This book encompasses both traditional and fresh new ways of connecting with the Goddesses and is intended as an introduction to the deities. You can use the book as a workbook, referring to it when you wish to celebrate the festivals and you can use the photographs as a focal point upon your altar. This book is intended to help bring the Goddesses to life, that they may enhance your life in the modern day.

There are many reasons why Goddesses are so popular in the modern spiritual world. For many it is a case of redressing the balance after centuries of patriarchal religion and they feel drawn to rediscover the 'old ways', hearkening back to a time when there was not just one God, but a multitude of Gods and Goddesses that govern all aspects of our lives.

The Wiccan belief is that of a Goddess and a God, who stand side by side, equal to each other. This concept is at the heart of this nature religion as the polarity of male and female is believed to be the key of life. Wicca's rapid growth in popularity within our modern world is testament to the widespread appeal of this concept to those who see it as a more appropriate model for modern life.

For others, the route to the Goddess has come through self-development and their quest for personal empowerment. Their journey often calls upon them to question their upbringing and conditioning and they often come to identify with a Divine Feminine principle, rather than the patriarchal divinities of mainstream religions. One way or another, ever since the Goddess movement took off during the middle of the twentieth century, women and men have been increasingly interested in exploring the concept of the Divine Feminine. Some people identify with only one Goddess, Mother Nature, the Earth. Others like to find the Goddess within themselves, to empower themselves and stand in their own power, maybe for the first time in their lives.

Priestesses tend to find their path to be a more devotional one, acknowledging individual Goddesses, seeking them out in the mythology of ancient times. Some Goddesses of the world are still very much alive within cultures, whilst others have been long forgotten by their people and eagerly await rediscovery.

Women and men frequently gather to celebrate the Goddess in ritual and song, awakening the Goddesses of many cultures and finding them alive and vibrant. If you are interested in exploring your spirituality then the Goddess energies are a good place to start. Their energies are accessible and responsive, benevolent and kind.

Working magically with the Goddess energies is effective because, quite simply, it works. When referring to magical practice, it is the ability to influence one's external surroundings with one's mind that is meant, also known as projecting one's True Will. Others refer to this as Cosmic Ordering or The Law of Attraction. We all have the capability to focus our minds and draw that which we desire towards us and in theory, we should be able attract anything we want towards us. But it's not always that easy.

Whereas it should not be necessary to employ the use of rituals and props in order to achieve results, in practice it can help immensely. This is partly due to the fact that we live in such a complicated world, full of external stimuli that constantly distract our minds. So if we replace one set of stimuli with another, then it can become a hypnotic trigger to achieve an altered state of consciousness quickly and effectively. Achieving a relaxed and deeper state of consciousness is essential to being able to project one's Will.

The whole point of any magical practice is to enhance your life, to be the best that you can be and to fulfil your true purpose in life, once you have discovered what that is. This is often referred to as finding your 'True Will', and is the meaning behind "Do what thou wilt shall be the whole of the Law" by Aleister Crowley. Knowing what you truly want is the key and if in doubt, connect with one of the Goddesses and ask to know what it is that you truly want. Then, once you are clear about your intentions, there is nothing stopping you from attracting them towards you. You can confidently create a sacred space, call upon the deity and ask for what you want, making sure you ask accurately for exactly what you want.

Working with the Goddess energies in magical practice adds power to the wishes and spells. Invoking the Goddesses also provides some extra guidance or insight into our own perceptions of your situation.

If we become accustomed to performing a ritual in our lives, it starts to become second nature. If we then start creating rituals that involve raising energy and altering our state of consciousness, then that too will become second nature. For some people, the word 'ritual' conjures up all sorts of dramatic connotations, usually rooted in horror films. Instead, think of all the rituals that are already in your everyday life and how they make you feel. It may be walking the dog at the same time every day, which in turn, creates a feeling that 'All is right with the world', or a favourite alcoholic tipple at the same time every evening, or a cup of tea whilst watching your favourite soap on television. You may notice that you instantly feel a certain way when repeating the ritual, quickly calm and relaxed or you feel a particular emotion.

So, if you then perform rituals which include the use of incenses, essential oils, mood enhancing music etc., then it is easy to achieve an altered state of consciousness quickly. Other factors can enhance the cosmic ordering process, the focussing of the will, such as performing the ritual at a particular moon phase, as the moon can act as an amplifier to your intentions. The inclusion of Goddesses in ritual practice is always beneficial, as they represent a higher energy source, a beneficial influence that can enhance a spell and guide the querent in a visualisation exercise.

Before commencing any of the exercises in this book, it is important to be aware of safety. When lighting candles, always ensure that they are placed safely away from anything that may catch fire. Make sure that the candles are secure in the candlestick, melting the bottom of the candle so that it sticks in the holder, if necessary. The visualisations often require that you light a candle before closing your eyes and going into a meditative state, so please do be sensible.

If you feel that the energies in your home and especially the space that you intend to work in are affected in any way by negativity, then you can cleanse the space as detailed below. When cleansing your space with salt and water, please take care not to sprinkle the water on anything electrical or surfaces that might be adversely affected by salt. A gentle sprinkling of the drops of water is sufficient, so please be sensible as to where you aim the water droplets.

When burning a sage smudge stick, always hold an ashtray beneath it as the embers can drop easily, running the risk of small burns. Please always ensure that the smudge stick is extinguished properly, this is sometimes difficult and may require running the smudge stick under the tap.

Space Clearing

Aim: To remove and clear negative energies or an atmosphere from your home. Can be useful after an upset.

Tools: Black candle, juniper, sage or rosemary oil, candlestick, rock salt, water, small bowl, sage smudge stick, Tibetan bells.

Add the rock salt to the water and sprinkle the water with your fingers around the room in a clockwise direction. (Please be careful of the electrical appliances, plugs etc.) As you do so, say;

"With this salt and this water I cleanse this space, may it be free from negativity, doubt and fear."

Light the sage smudge stick and direct the smoke into all the corners of the room. As you do so, say:

"With this sage, I cleanse the energy of this room, I remove all residue of negative energies."

Take your Tibetan bells and ring them, and as they sound say:

"Let this space be cleared of any trapped energies, may these sound vibrations remove all negativity, doubt and fear."

Now take your black candle and anoint it with the oil. Focus on the candle and say:

"As this candle burns, I burn away all negative energies, may they be gone forever. I banish ... (detail what it is that you wish to be rid of, e.g. the residue of emotions after an upset). So mote it be!" Light your candle and place it in the candlestick. Let it burn all the way down.

Cleansing Bath

Take a bath with rock salt and three drops each of sage, rosemary and juniper oils. Visualise yourself being cleansed of all negativity, whether it comes from oneself or another.

Creating a Sacred Space

Aim: To prepare the space for ritual work or visualisations with Goddesses.

Tools: Rock salt, water, small bowl, incense, meditation music, white altar candle.

Cleanse the space as detailed above if necessary. If the energies do not need to be cleared, then simply sprinkle salt and water around the room and say:

"With this salt and this water, I cleanse this space. May it be free from negativity, doubt and fear."

Light your incense and put on some soft meditation music. Light your altar candle. Close your eyes and visualise a halo of light around the candle flame. See it growing larger, growing as it expands until it becomes a golden ball of pulsating light. It becomes larger and larger, filling up the whole room. As it envelops you, you are at once free from all negativity, doubt and fear. It fills up the whole property and expands to the boundaries of the property. Now visualise the light from the candle flame coming towards

you as a stream of light, and it illuminates your aura, making your energy bright and clear, vibrant and protected. You are safe within this sacred space. Now you can begin your ritual.

IMBOLC
Brighid

*"Brighid of the flaming hair, Lady of Healing
we seek nourishment from your healing well,
that we may recover and renew our strength.
We nurture your sacred flame of inspiration,
and ask for your guidance, that we may forge our tools.
Great Brighid, join us as we celebrate your day"*

Imbolc is an ancient Celtic fire festival celebrated on February the 2nd. The word Imbolc means 'in the belly', that is, it represents the first stirring of spring in the womb of Mother Earth. Another name for this celebration is Candlemas as it is customary for many candles to be lit in honour of this time, and some traditions continue whereby a young maiden wears a crown of lit candles to represent the spirit of the season.

Brighid is a Celtic Goddess most often associated with Ireland. She is the Goddess of the Well and the Spring but also of Fire. It is unusual for a Goddess to be associated with two elements, but Brighid is, as she is the Goddess of the Forge and of Blacksmiths. As the guardian of holy wells, she is very popular in Glastonbury, famous for its sacred Chalice Well.

According to legend, it is said that when an old crone drank from Brighid's Well of Youth, she was transformed into Brighid, the beautiful Virgin Goddess.

This Goddess is known by many variations of her name; Brigantia, Brigit, Brigadonia, Brighid, Brid, Bride, Bridie, Brigan, Brigandu and Braid. All of these names mean 'The Most High'. She was later adopted by the Christian church and became known as Saint Bridget.

In Irish mythology, Brighid is a Triple Goddess, being one of three triplets, all sisters and all named Brighid. Their father was the All-Father God, and their mother a mortal woman from an early tribe of Ireland. As a Triple Goddess, the three aspects of Brighid were as the Goddesses of Healing, Poetry and Smithcraft. In her aspect as Goddess of Poetry, she provides inspiration for all bards, writers, poets and artists who can call upon her to help in these creative endeavours today.

She is also a midwife, a compassionate mother and protector of the hearth and home. Her son, who was a smith, and who had taught her the smith's art, was killed in battle and as she mourned for him, she wailed and wailed so loudly that her cries could be heard across all the land. This was the first time that cries had been heard in Ireland. Brighid, who was also a metal-smith, created a special kind of whistle and its high, piercing sound would enable people to find each other in the dark.

Brighid is sometimes depicted as having two sides to her face, one ugly and the other very beautiful. This identifies her with the Irish Saint, Bridget of Kildare, which is a Christianised version of the Goddess. Saint Bridget had prayed to be made ugly so that she could dedicate herself to God – but when she took her vows, she was made beautiful again. It is said that St Bridget also invented the tradition of women being allowed to propose to men on a Leap Year.

As a Fire Goddess and Warrior, she can be vengeful if wrongs have been done, especially to women, and she will utter shrill cries of despair. This warrior aspect of her was very prevalent in Scotland where she was the primary deity of the Brigantes tribe and she was known as Brigantia, who lent her name to Great Britain. The image of Brigantia as the Goddess of Great Britain is still used today.

Brighid brings the gift of milk to all creatures and has a sacred white cow as her totem animal. Her festival is Imbolc, (February the 1st or 2nd) which is the time that animals start to lactate. Her fire brings the first stirrings of life to the Earth and is also the time of year when the days begin to noticeably lengthen as the light is returning to the world. Therefore Brighid became known as the 'bringer of the light', and is often depicted holding a flame or wearing a crown of candles. She represents renewal in all things, in the ever-turning sequence of the seasons.

Although she is a Fertility Goddess and protector of new brides, she is also patroness of virgins and feminists. According to myths it is claimed that Saint Bridget's convent was surrounded by a magical hedge which was so powerful that no man could touch it or cross over it.

Call upon the Goddess Brighid to help you find inspiration in your work, especially writing, poetry and the arts. As she is also the Goddess of the Forge, you can ask for assistance in forging your plans into reality, bringing together ideas. As the midwife and mother, she can help you to give birth to new ideas and projects and protect them as they flourish and grow. As a healer, she can bless you with healing, all you need to do is to ask and she will illuminate the way forward with her flame.

Bride's Bed

Rushes, oak and white flowers are sacred to Brighid. To call Brighid into your home on Candlemas Day, or Imbolc, prepare a 'Bride's Bed'. This is usually a shallow basket, made of rushes (a wickerwork basket such as for floristry displays is ideal). Line the basket with reeds or rushes if possible, or any kind of greenery. Add some sprigs of oak and decorate the whole thing with white flowers. Make a Bride doll out of raffia, and decorate her with white lace, linen or paper. Set aside a table on which a white cloth has been draped. The Bride and her bed are placed on this altar, in between two white candles. Have some light incense burning and when you are ready to call Brighid, place her in her bed and light both candles, saying: "Brid is come! Brid is welcome!" Leave her there for one or two nights. If you have any jewellery, such as an engagement or wedding ring, that you would like her to bless, place it in the bed with her. She will also bless agricultural implements, gardening tools, kitchen or needlework items, if you leave them close to the altar.

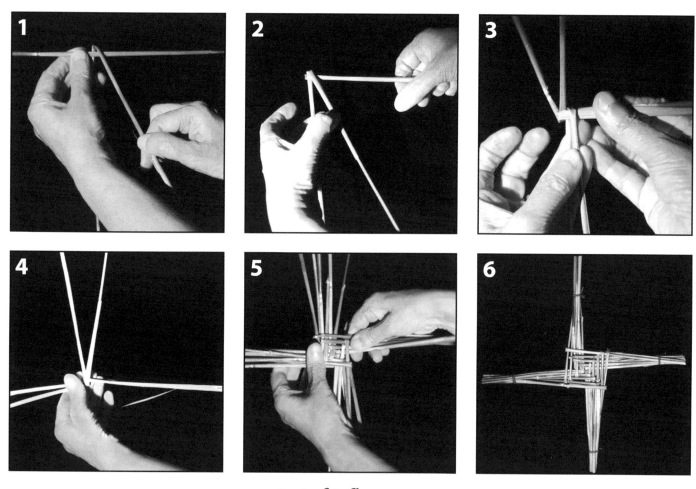

Brighid's Cross
By Seldiy Bate

To bless your home and invite Brighid in, on the night of Candlemas, strew rushes or straw from your front door and into the house. Leave some grass outside for her sacred cow. You may place a Brighid Cross over the hearth, or a small one in each room.

A Brighid Cross is traditionally made of rushes, but wheat straws look very attractive. If you have collected some corn at the harvest time and kept it from the previous year, you can weave the straws into a Brighid Cross. You may be able to buy some dried corn or wheat from a floristry supply shop, if not, craft shops sell paper straws and these also look nice and are easier to use. Natural straws should be wrapped up in a towel and soaked in water for a couple of hours. Twenty-eight long straws make a nicely proportioned design, but you can use less.

Hold two straws in an equal-armed cross, with the horizontal one in front. Fold the vertical one down, making a T shape. Turn anti-clockwise, so that the top bar of the T becomes vertical and fold the top part of it down. Turn it anti-clockwise again and add a vertical straw behind the horizontal and to the right of the vertical arm, fold it down. Turn anti-clockwise and add another straw, as before. Keep turning and adding straws, keeping the weave regular, with the straws side by side. Build the cross until you are happy with the size and tie the four arms off with raffia or red silk or wool. Trim the ends. The Brighid Cross represents the turning of the seasons and the balance of the elements and will bring the protection of Brighid into your home.

Imbolc Oil

- $1/4$ oz base carrier oil
- 4 drops eucalyptus oil
- 5 drops frankincense oil
- 3 drops geranium oil
- 5 drops ginger oil
- 5 drops lavender oil
- 10 drops neroli oil
- jasmine flowers

Instructions
- Add the drops of oil to the base oil using a dropper
- Add the flowers and shake well.
- Meditate upon the Goddess Brighid and ask her to bless the oil.

Visualisation

Aim: For Inspiration and help with work, to ask for growth with your projects, for healing and restoration.

Tools: Statue or photo of Brighid, white candle, snowdrops, candlestick, and Imbolc oil

Incense: Jasmine.

Create a sacred space as detailed in Chapter One. Light your incense and place by your statue / photo. Place your snowdrops on the altar. Call upon the Goddess Brighid:

"Brighid of the flaming hair, Lady of Healing,
We call upon you to join us at this time of Imbolc.
We seek nourishment from your healing well,
That we may recover and renew our strength.
We nurture your sacred flame of inspiration,
And ask for your guidance, that we may forge our tools.
Great Brighid, join us as we celebrate your day."

Now take your white candle and anoint it with the Imbolc oil. Focus on your candle and ask aloud that which you desire. Ask the Goddess to grant this to you and to show you the way to forge ahead with your plans. Light your candle, say: "So mote it be!" and place it safely in a candlestick. Now close your eyes and see the flame burning brightly in your mind's eye. As you focus on the flame, you become aware of two hands holding the flame within. You look up to find yourself gazing into the face of the most beautiful Goddess, fair of face, with flowing red locks. She smiles, and you gaze into her beautiful deep blue eyes, feeling the healing energy emanating from within. She asks you that which you would desire and you tell her, asking her for her guidance on how best to achieve this. If it is healing that you seek, you ask her what practical steps you may take to enhance the process; if it is inspiration and work that you desire, ask her how best to go about it. Listen to her wise words, perhaps she will give you a gift. She beckons to a well beside her, the Chalice Well, the heart of the spring, surrounded by snowdrops. She pulls up a ribbon from within the well. You see a chalice attached to it, brimming with beautiful spring water, glistening in the winter light. She offers it to you and you drink from the waters. You feel the healing powers of the waters coursing through you, invigorating you, refreshing you, replenishing your spirit. Hand the chalice back to Brighid and thank her for her blessing. At this moment you notice a movement above you and you look up as a swan flies overhead. You take your leave of the Goddess and walk towards the bright sun and step into the light, through the light until you see yourself once again before your altar, with the flame of the white candle burning brightly. Bring your awareness back into your body and wiggle your toes. Open your eyes in your own time and let your candle burn all the way down.

Healing Dew Spell

On February the 1st in the evening lay a white sheet out on the grass. Light a white candle anointed with Imbolc oil and call upon the Goddess Brighid to come and bless you:

"Light the fires of inspiration in my heart that I may speak with words that reflect
Your healing wisdom." [i]

Let the candle burn all the way down. Early the following morning, go and collect the sheet whilst it is still wet with the dew. Give thanks to the Goddess for her healing and her blessings. The fabric moistened by the dew will contain the healing properties of the Goddess, you can cover yourself with it or cut it into smaller pieces and give them to those who need healing.

A Traditional Manx Prayer to Bring Brighid's Blessings to Your Home:

Create a sacred space as detailed in Chapter One. Light a white candle, anointed with lily of the valley or orange blossom oil. Place them before your picture or statue of Brighid. Collect some snowdrops and place then in a small vase as an offering to the Goddess.

"Brid, Brid, come to my house,
Come to my house tonight!
Brid, Brid, come, O come
To my house tonight!
O open you the door to Brid,
Let Brid come in.
Brid, Brid, come you
To my house tonight!" [ii]

Persephone

"Hail Persephone, Goddess of the gates of life and death, who dwells in a beautiful Spring garden amongst the shadows of the *Underworld*. In your left hand you hold a *pomegranate*, the fruit of Hades, your voice is a low call heard at evening, luring those who hear you to *deep dreams*. You await us at the gate between the worlds, that there might be a *sweet welcome* for life as it passes into death, and a light, swift welcome for death as it passes into life; at every *spring* you shall return to us, and gladden the Earth with birdsong, and refresh the mind and eye with *innocence*, so that a new tale may unfold with the coming year. *(iii)*

P ersephone is the Greek Goddess of Youthfulness and Springtime. She is represented as a maiden and a virgin, as she is the daughter of Demeter, Goddess of Agriculture. However, she also has another aspect, which is Mistress of the Dead, due to her link with the Underworld. She has two main aspects; when she is the girl-like daughter of the Corn Goddess, she is known as Kore; but after she has spent time with Hades in the Underworld as his Queen, she is known as Persephone and the Mistress of the Dead. These two aspects are linked in her myth, which also tells of her mother Demeter, who is explored in more depth in the chapter on Lammas. Demeter and Persephone lived very happily together and as a result of this, the Earth was always abundant with fruits and crops and it was the season of summer all year long. Hades, the God of the Underworld, saw how happy they were and as he studied them, he became very attracted to Peresphone. He wanted her for himself and made plans to take her for his lover. Hades abducted Persephone and took her down into the Underworld, where he raped her and held her captive.

On the Earth, Demeter was distraught and she mourned the loss of her beloved daughter. She searched the world for her, helped by the Goddess Hecate, but despite their searching, they could find no trace of Persephone. The search continued endlessly and Demeter began to neglect the crops because she was so intent upon finding her daughter. Everything in the fields withered and died. Eventually, the world was in such a sorry state that Demeter's husband, Zeus, intervened and ordered that Hades release Persephone immediately. Hades agreed to this, but only on the condition that she had eaten nothing whilst she was in Underworld. Demeter was so overjoyed to be reunited with her daughter that the Earth immediately became abundant again and the crops began to grow. However, Persephone confessed that during her time with Hades, she had eaten six pomegranate seeds. Therefore, Zeus ruled that for six months of every year, Persephone must return to the Underworld and live with Hades. Every year, when she descended, Demeter would mourn for her daughter once more and the plant life would die. Then, every spring, when she emerged from the Underworld, Demeter would be happy and the plants would grow again. This became the myth explaining the change in the seasons as Persephone descends to the Underworld in autumn and returns again in spring. Symbolically Persephone is viewed as the corn, which must descend into the earth so that from her apparent death new fruit may germinate and provide the harvest for the coming year.

It is worth looking again at the relationship between Demeter and Persephone, as Demeter was quite possibly a rather controlling mother, who thought she knew what was best for daughter, especially her choice of suitors. Hades may not have kidnapped and raped Persephone at all, she may have gone with him of her own free will. She may have found him attractive and preferred his company to those of the young men being selected for her by her mother. After all, it wouldn't be the first time that the young impressionable girl was seduced by the excitement and danger of a man who was known as a 'bad boy'.

Alternatively, there were many tales of ancient Greek love magic, binding spells that a man could use to seduce a woman. Perhaps it was one such spell that Hades employed to bring the beautiful Persephone to his bed? The love spell had many variations but all involved the use of a fruit with seeds in, such as an apple, a pomegranate or a melon. The man would recite an incantation three times over the fruit:

"I shall strike with apples (or pomegranates or melons), I shall give this potion, always timely and edible to mortal men and immortal Gods. To whichever woman I give or at whichever woman I throw this apple or hit with it, setting everything aside, may she be mad for my love, whether she takes it in her hand and eats it…or sets it in her bosom and may she not stop loving me. O Lady Cyprogeneia, bring to perfection this perfect incantation!"

This spell ends with the traditional asking of Aphrodite (Cyprogeneia) to bring the spell to fulfilment. Another version cites:

"You give the fruit to the woman and she sucks the juices. That woman will come to you and you can make love to her."

It is believed that Hades cast a variation of this spell on Persephone before she returned to Demeter, to control her desire and ensure that she returned to him. In the Homeric hymn to Demeter, we see that Persephone claims that Hades performed some kind of 'binding magic' to bind her to him, having secretly consecrated the seeds of the pomegranate:

"Demeter was answered by Persephone, the most beautiful: "So then, Mother, I shall tell you everything, without error. When the messenger came to me, the swift Mercury (Argos)-killer, with the news from my father, the son of Cronus (Kronos), and from the other dwellers in the sky that I should come from Erebos, so that you may see me with your own eyes and let go of your grief and terrible wrath against the immortals, then I sprang up for joy, but Hades, stealthily, put into my hand the berry of the pomegranate, that honey-sweet food, and he compelled me by order to eat of it."

Working with Persephone can help you to descend into your inner self, to examine the darker issues in your life. Looking at uncomfortable situations can give you a greater insight and understanding of yourself. Then you can re–emerge once again into your outer world, feeling restored and renewed. It is also good to work with this Goddess if you wish to gain a greater understanding of your relationship with your mother, perhaps she has been too controlling or it was difficult to gain her approval. You can also ask Persephone to aid growth in new projects and new relationships.

Imbolc spell

Aim: To encourage new growth in your life.
Tools: Photo or statue of Persephone, a white and light green candle.
Incense: Jasmine or lily of the valley.

Light your incense in front of Persephone, say:

"In this rite we remember the Goddess who left us in the autumn. Return to us, maiden, and bring with you the spring, that we may experience renewal in our lives. The plants that dwell beneath the earth make ready their reappearance, great Goddess Persephone, maiden, we ask that you return to us, bring with you the spring."

Persephone Spell
By Seldiy Bate

AIM: To boost self-esteem and be appreciated. When Persephone dwells in the Underworld, she is unseen. And yet she is honoured and loved there. When she returns to the Upper World, the whole of Nature awakens and rejoices. Do you sometimes feel unappreciated? Perhaps you don't believe in your own worth? Or maybe you want recognition for who you are, what you do, perhaps a work or career situation, where you want some credit? Do this spell to bring out the appreciation of you.

Drape a table with a black or dark coloured cloth. Over this, lay a strip of gold cloth, vertically down the centre. Metallic gold is nice, if you have it (a long scarf would work). You will need some appropriate incense, such as mastic, or, if using a joss stick or oil burner, lily, narcissus or mint. Have a vase of flowers, lilies or narcissi are appropriate, and a maroon candle in a holder. You will need a photograph of yourself, a small square of black or brown cloth (larger than the photo) and a rock or large stone. Place the photograph in the centre of the table and the cloth and rock to one side. You will be calling upon Persephone's aspect as the hidden Goddess, so it is customary not to name her. Although this is a Persephone spell, do not use this name during your working. When you are ready to begin, get the incense going, then light the candle, saying:

"I call upon you, secret Queen,
Return to us again
That the Upper World may see your beauty,
Feel your magic,
Know your worth!"

Now pick up your photograph and hold it up, with the picture facing the altar, say: "Lady of the Dark Realms, this is me, (your name)."

Now express in your own words what it is that is making you feel undervalued. Tell her what it is you wish to say and ask of those who may be taking advantage of you, or making you feel disrespected. Whatever the problem is, tell her, she is listening.

Now put the photograph back on the altar and cover it with the cloth, say: "Hidden, yet there always!"

Place the rock on top of the cloth.

"Blocked, but not always!"

Think about the way you have been blocked and recall how Persephone, although taken to the Underworld, was permitted to return to the light. Give yourself permission to be loved and valued as you remove the rock and place it to one side.

Cry: "We are set free!"

Remove the cloth and toss it to one side.

Cry: "The light shines on you and me!"

Hold your photograph towards the candle flame and say:

"Lady of the Light, even when imprisoned in the gloom,
You were always there for all.
You were always loved, even by the darkness.
Now you are free, returned to the land and loved by the light.
So may light shine upon me
And I be respected for my worth!"

"I thank you, Queen of Returning Light, restored to the World!"

Extinguish the candle, you may burn it any time until it is used up. Keep your photo somewhere where you can look at it often and tell yourself you are loved and appreciated!

Visualisation / Ritual

Aim: To understand a difficult or dark situation and to release it. To see things more positively, to let go of negativity in your life and move forwards.

Tools: Statue or photo of Persephone, green candle, black candle, two candlesticks.

Incense: Lily of the valley or jasmine.

Offerings: Pomegranate or pomegranate juice, flowers.

Create a sacred space as detailed in Chapter One. Light your incense and your candles and place them safely on the candlesticks. Place the flowers on the altar. Call upon the Goddess Persephone:

"Great Goddess Persephone, I call to you to be here present at this rite.

As you descended to the Underworld, I ask that I be able to descend into my inner self and to know my truth and reconnect with my own feeling of self-worth. Then, shall I rise again and return to my outer world, so that I may act upon this knowledge and make my desires manifest. Accept these offerings of incense and pomegranate."

Close your eyes and see the burning flames of the two candles in front of you. Imagine yourself walking through a wood, with dappled light filtering though the trees, as you proceed you find yourself in an area of light, then an area of shade, then light then shade. As you wander deeper into the wood, you find yourself enveloped in darkness and shade, until you come across the opening of a cave. You sit awhile on a rock near the mouth of the cave and consider that which is dark in your life. Is there something in your life that you would like to leave behind? Perhaps something about yourself: old habits, old patterns, emotions or attitudes? After a while you notice a movement from the cave entrance, and Persephone emerges from the cave as the sun breaks through the trees, casting dappled light around you both. She holds the pomegranate towards you and invites you to take it. As you take it she also takes your hand and leads you into the deep into the

22

cave. You wander a little way into the cave and she asks you about the darkness in your life and what you would like to leave behind. Discuss this with her and partake of the pomegranate fruit. How many seeds do you eat? After a while, when you feel that you are ready to leave behind your darkness, ask Persephone to show you the way out and into the light. She takes you by the hand and leads you out of the cave and into the dappled light of a sunny clearing. You walk together through the wooded glade, and she tells you what is to come for you, how to leave the darkness behind and re-enter the light. Tell her what you would like to achieve and she will guide you toward it. As you come to the edge of the woodland, you find yourself feeling refreshed, re-energised and feeling lighter than before. You take your leave of Persephone, thanking her for her guidance and her blessings, safe in the knowledge that you can return to see her at any time. As you walk away from the woodland, towards the sun, bring your awareness back into your room and see yourself sitting or lying in your meditation, with your candles before you. Bring your awareness back into your body and wiggle your toes and in your own time open your eyes. Raise your glass of pomegranate juice or take some of the pomegranate and hold it before the Goddess, say: "Beautiful Goddess Persephone, I honour you with this offering and thank you for your blessings." Drink /eat some of the offering and say: "Hail Persephone!" After you have partaken of the offering, address the Goddess once again: "Beautiful Goddess Persephone, I thank you for being here with me today. Until the next time I bid you hail and farewell!" Let your candles burn all the way down.

Blessed Persephone, fair *maiden* divine,

Come, blessed queen, and to these rites incline:

Goddess of Spring, whose holy form in *budding fruits* we honour you,

Hear us, blessed Goddess, send a rich increase

Of various fruits from earth, with lovely Peace;

Bless us with health and crown my life

With *blest abundance*, free from noisy strife;

Dismiss we willing to the realms beneath,

To thy fair palace, where happy *spirits dwell*, and Hades reigns. (iv)

OSTARA
Spring Equinox

Ostara! *Queen of the Spring*, Returned from the dark land of Death,

The cold Earth grows warm with your breath, your breath of life.

Be kind to me Gentle Goddess, I have not killed the *hare before his season*.

Be kind to me Gentle Goddess, I have not worked the Magics

In thy name without reason.

Ostara! Child of the Dawn!

Who causes the *flowers* to *grow with love*.

Ostara! Mother of Life!

Kindle the *Equinox Fires*, The spirit, the hopes, the *desires*,

Of women and men.

'Hymn to Ostara' by Seldiy Bate

The Spring Equinox is celebrated on March the 21st, and is one of two times during the year when the day and the night are exactly the same length. In some cultures, such as the Babylonians, it was believed to have been the time of year when the world was created, therefore it was seen as the start of the new year. This Equinox is also known as the Vernal Equinox.

Ostara is the Goddess of Spring and is celebrated at the time of the Spring Equinox. There are many different variations of her name, in Old English she was known as Eostre or Eastre, whilst the name Ostara originates from the Old Germanic language. They are all names attributed to the Anglo-Saxon Goddess of Spring, from whose name the Christian Festival of Easter is also derived.

As the Goddess of the Spring Equinox, her name has been taken for the Wiccan festival of Ostara, which is the time of the Spring Equinox. It is believed that at this time of year, the Goddess brings new life and fertility to the land. This is when life returns and begins to flourish again, the advent of spring.

Ostara is also known as the Goddess of the Rising Sun and the Dawn, because the Equinox marks the point when the days will start to lengthen and become warmer. It is the point when the balance shifts from the cold winter when nature dies, to the warmth of summer and new growth.

At this time the Goddess first takes form as a bright star which rises in the east and then becomes a beautiful maiden, enveloped in golden light. As Ostara rises up into the sky, beams of light accompany her and they turn into animals. Ostara's totem animal is the hare, often linked with this time of year as a fertility symbol for thousands of years. The leaping hare is a symbol associated with joy, suggestive of the dance of life, as the light and warmth return to the land. Hares mate in the spring and at this time, display frenzied courtship behaviour (mad March hares). Because hares were superseded by rabbits in the twelfth century in Britain, it is the rabbit which has now become associated with the Festival of Spring, Easter in Christian tradition, i.e. the "Easter Bunny".

At Easter festival, it is traditional to celebrate with an egg, either an egg hunt or the more modern chocolate Easter eggs. This symbol originates with the Goddess Ostara and is a symbol of rebirth. She is often depicted holding an egg, as this Goddess holds the promise of new life. There is a mystery to the egg, as it represents the everlasting circle of life, leading to the eternal question of 'which came first, the chicken or the egg?' However, the egg held by Ostara is believed to be a snake's egg, because this was always a symbol of rebirth in ancient times.

There is a legend that tells of Ostara finding a wounded bird and the only way she could save it was to turn it into a hare. So the hare became her companion, but it was still able to lay eggs. Other variations of the myth say that the bird was the God of Winter, who had been hunted and he was unable to escape because of the cold. Ostara saved him and by turning him into a hare, gave him a new lease of life. She allowed him to lay rainbow coloured eggs because she was the Goddess of many coloured flowers. Children still hunt for multi-coloured eggs in traditional Easter games. The egg symbol also represents the yoni, the creative power of the

Great Mother, and this image is represented on more traditional versions of the World Tarot card. According to myth, if you break an egg accidentally at the time of the Spring Equinox, it is a sign from Ostara, that she is promising something new. This could be good luck, love, or abundance. It is an indication that she is promising you that something new and positive will manifest.

On the morning of the Spring Equinox it is said that Ostara arrives and brings the new growth of the plant life. It is believed that wherever she walks, new flowers begin to grow beneath her feet. Therefore, the winter landscape begins to change as the plants awaken and spring arrives.

Call upon the Goddess Ostara if you wish to cultivate new growth in your life, or to bring an idea or project from conception to birth, to actuality. Ask her for the power and confidence to create all that is new in your life, with her blessing and ask that the results may flourish and grow, bringing you joy and delight.

Ostara Incense

- 2 parts frankincense
- 1 part Benzoin
- $\frac{1}{2}$ part nutmeg
- 1 drop jasmine oil
- $\frac{1}{2}$ part orange peel
- $\frac{1}{2}$ part rose petals

Instructions
- Grind the ingredients with a mortar and pestle
- Burn on a charcoal block in a fire safe burner

Balancing Spell

Aim: To honour spring and to attain balance.

Tools: Some old leaves, one for each thing that you wish to get rid of. Some seeds or seedlings, one for each new thing that you wish to manifest in your life.

Call upon the Goddess Ostara and ask her to be present for this rite. Dig a hole large enough for the seedlings that you wish to grow. Write on each of the dead leaves something that you wish to get rid of from your life. Then place the dead leaves in the bottom of the hole and say: "Great Goddess Ostara, Lady of the Equinox, Goddess of Balance, please accept these things that I wish to be rid of. As these leaves rot and nourish the earth, I release these negative blocks that have been holding me back."

Now place the seedlings on top of the leaves, one for each thing that you wish to manifest and say: "Ostara, please accept these wishes which I want to manifest in my life during the coming season. Let them flourish and grow as they take their strength from the rotted remains of that which has gone before. So mote it be!"

Then thank the Goddess Ostara for her blessings.

Affirming Your Attributes

Write a list of ten of your plus points, things you are good at, and ten minus points, things you would like to improve, taking care to be honest and not to be overly critical of yourself, especially when it comes to physical attributes.

Light a light green candle, anointed with geranium oil. Read aloud one point from one list followed by one point from the other, until you have read all aloud and say:

"Here I stand at the pivotal point. May I always have a balanced view of my attributes and my flaws. May I follow a path of balance as I walk between the two, always appreciating my attributes and seeking to improve my flaws. So mote it be!"

Visualisation / Ritual

Aim: To bring about balance in your life.
Tools: Statue or photo of Ostara, tea light and holder, light green candle, lilac candle, candlesticks.
Oils: Lavender and geranium.
Incense: Jasmine, rose or Ostara incense.

Create a sacred space as detailed in Chapter One. Light the incense and the tea light in front of your statue or photo of Ostara. Call upon the Goddess:

"I call to you, O fertile Goddess, you who are heavy with child. Great Ostara, as you run with the hares, I call to you to be here now, join us in this rite at this time of Vernal Equinox. Bring balance into our lives and guide us, so that we may give birth to all that is new and abundant in our lives. Help us to create that which we desire, to nourish all that is good in our lives. Aid us in nurturing the tender buds of our success, of our endeavours, of our loves and in our lives. Bestow your blessings upon us and help us so that they may blossom and grow. Great Goddess Ostara, I bid you hail and welcome!"

Take your green candle and anoint it with geranium oil. As you do so, say aloud that which you wish to bring into your life, ask for the nourishment, abundance and growth that you desire, to cultivate that which is tender and young in your life, to strengthen that which is weak. Ask for balance to be restored wherever there may be imbalance. Light your candle, say: "So mote it be!" and place it in the candlestick.

Take your lilac candle and anoint it with lavender oil. Focus upon it and ask for healing and equilibrium, mentally, spiritually and physically. Ask for balance to be restored wherever it is needed, for issues to be resolved and for the path ahead to be shown clearly. Light your candle and say: "So mote it be!"

Close your eyes and focus your mind upon your altar, imagine yourself walking through a wooded glade, with dappled sunlight breaking through the trees. All around the shoots of spring are breaking through the leaves of the woodland floor. You can see fresh new green leaves upon the trees and feel a light breeze in the air. A rustling noise to the side of the clearing startles you, as you look up you see a hare sitting looking back at you. The hare hops towards

you and then she emerges from the thick forest, long flowing hair adorned with wild flowers, her radiant skin aglow with natural beauty, her belly swollen with child.

Behold Ostara, expectant mother, Goddess of Spring. She walks with you through the forest, accompanied by the hare that hops along beside you, sometimes going ahead, then waiting as you both catch up. The hare leads you both further into the forest and stops by a large tree trunk that has fallen on to its side during a storm. The Goddess gestures for you to reach your hand into the side of the tree trunk, where it has split with age and as you do, you find a small nest made of moss. You can feel something hard and round in the nest. Ostara encourages you to retrieve it, you pick it up and pull out a smooth white egg. The Goddess talks to you about what this egg represents to you. Then as you both walk back from whence you came she explains how things will come to pass in your future. At the edge of the woodland glade she stops, explaining that you must now return to bring your desires to life, just as she too must soon give birth to her child. You take your leave of her, safe in the knowledge that you can return at any time and make your way towards the sun, glowing with a golden light and sitting low in the sky. As you walk into the light, you find yourself once again in your room, aware of yourself sitting before your altar with the candles burning brightly. Bring your awareness back into your body and wiggle your toes. In your own time, open your eyes. Thank the Goddess Ostara for her blessings and guidance and bid her: "Hail and farewell!" Let your candles burn all the way down.

BELTANE

The Green Lady and the Horned God

Beltane!
I dance with *delight* on Beltane's night.
All senses freeing, I dance for being.
The flower and the *flame* of *love's own rite* shall blossom. [i]
From "Hedge Witch" by Rae Beth

Beltane is celebrated on May Eve, April the 30th and May Day, May the 1st. It is an Ancient Celtic fire festival, which marks the beginning of the lighter half of the year. The name means 'bright fire' and in ancient times fires would be lit on the hilltops. Fragrant boughs, such as juniper, were thrown onto the fires, to appease the Gods and bring purification and protection. Cattle would be driven in between two fires, to bring fertility and people would even pass through or jump over the fires, in order to attract good luck or to become pregnant in the coming year.

The Green Lady is a Goddess of Nature, and is often regarded as the spirit of the woods, the hedgerows and fields, everywhere that green plants flourish. She is seen as the magical force of Nature as she bestows life to all growing things. Like many Goddesses, she is seen to hold the key to life and death, for as all vegetation grows, so must it die, before re-emerging in a new life cycle the following year.

In Ancient Europe, there were many cults that worshipped a Green Goddess, honouring her at a sacred grove of trees. The legends would tell of a Green Goddess who was sought after and pursued by a Horned God, also represented as a Green Man. Some myths tell of the Green Goddess being magically transformed into a tree as she is chased by the Horned God. This would be re-enacted by priests dressed in animal skins, wearing antlers on their heads. By doing this, they take on the personification of the Horned God and would seek to invoke his energy during Beltane rites.

We find another version of this myth in Greek legend where the nymph Daphne was magically transformed into a laurel tree. The laurel tree was regarded as sacred to the Goddess, largely due to the hallucinogenic properties of its leaves. In ceremonies, a priestess would chew the leaves from the laurel tree and as the hallucinogen affected her, she would go into a trance and have visions, believed to be prophecies. She would then deliver the oracle of the Goddess to the assembled company. Therefore it was believed that the laurel tree bestowed the inspiration of the Goddess upon those that honoured her. In keeping with other Green Goddess traditions, Daphne was a green nymph, a nymph of the land, and she was sought after by the sun God Apollo. Interestingly, Apollo is also sometimes depicted as having horns upon his head. Not wishing to be caught, Daphne ran away from Apollo and sought the help of the Goddess Gaia, Goddess of the Earth. Gaia helped Daphne by transforming her into the laurel tree.

As the Green Lady appears many times within European mythology, so we also find the Green Man. He is depicted as a man clothed only in green foliage and he appears to 'breathe' leaves as they are seen to be coming from his nostrils and mouth. Sometimes the Green Man is also depicted with horns or branches, symbolising antlers, which were an indication of his wild and animalistic nature. Green Man images are more common and have survived in folk customs, art and architecture and it is possible to see many Green Man images carved in church architecture.

The Horned God is the God of Nature and is represented as a man with horns or antlers on his head and sometimes even an animal's head. The Horned God is the personification of the life force energy in wild animals and he represents the divine masculine principle, being both equal and opposite to the feminine, the Goddess. The Horned God is linked with the sun as his antlers symbolise reaching up towards the Sun. He is honoured at Beltane as it is at this time of year that the warmth of the sun can be felt once again, and the sun's rays bring life back to the earth. He is the Consort to the Goddess, and he pursues her in an endless cycle of birth, life, death and

rebirth. Many myths tell how the Horned God pursues the Goddess of Nature, the Green Lady. He often catches her and they join together in a fruitful union. However, she is destined to destroy him, only to give birth to him again as the Wheel of the Year turns and the cycle comes full circle.

The Horned God is also known as Cernunnos, a Celtic deity with antlers. Cernunnos is often shown sitting in a meditative position and surrounded by wild animals. He is also linked to Herne the Hunter, another Horned God, who is thought to have been derived from Cernunnos, but Herne was only really known around the region of the Windsor Forest and its surrounding areas in Berkshire, England.

In the Ancient Roman mythology, the Horned God is represented as Pan, and he is the God of the Wild Woods and the herds that roam within them. He is depicted as having horns upon his head and the hindquarters of a goat. Pan is a known to be a God with a very healthy and lusty appetite and he is always pursuing young nymphs or anyone that takes his fancy.

The horns may also be seen as a symbol of abundance and wealth for in ancient times they were used as drinking horns. Therefore, the role of the Horned God becomes that of the provider. He is also known as the Lord of Death and Rebirth because the Horned God is believed to carry the souls of the dead to the Underworld, also known as the Summerland, where they await rebirth.

Call upon the Green Lady and the Horned God if you are seeking a new love in your life, or if you wish to become pregnant. Perhaps you have a relationship or project where you feel the passion has diminished and you wish to resuscitate it. You can ask the Green Lady and the Horned God to reawaken the fires of passion once again.

Beltane Spell

Aim: To connect with the Green Goddess and Horned God, to manifest that which you desire.
Tools: Statues or pictures of the Green Lady and Horned God, tea lights and holders, wooden wand, cedar or sandalwood oil, green candle, candlestick, small dish, earth, some wild flowers.
Incense: Cedar.

To make a wooden wand, firstly take wood from the ground, not from a living tree. Cut the wood into the shape of a phallus or find a simple branch and peel off the bark. Place the wand upon your altar. Place some earth in the small dish and place it on the altar by the wand. Create a sacred space as detailed in Chapter One, light the incense and the tea lights in front of the statues or pictures, and call upon the Green Lady and the Horned God:

"I call to you, Green Lady of the Wood, honour me with your presence at this time of Beltane. Green Lady we ask that you are

Herne the Hunter

present at this rite. Hail and welcome! Great Horned God, I call to you, consort of the Green Lady. Great Horned God, at this time of fertility and love, we bid you hail and welcome!"

Light the candle to the Sun. This represents the fire of Beltane, which serves as an invocation to the Sun God and it represents purification and protection. When you light your candle ponder upon these qualities and symbolism, say:

"I light this candle in honour of the Sun God. May it represent your protective and healing power."

Now take up a dish of earth. Bless it in the name of the Green Lady. Touch the earth with your hands and say:

"May this earth be sacred in honour of the Green Lady. May it be imbued with nurturing life giving power."

Decorate the dish of earth with flowers. Now, take a wooden wand and anoint it with the cedar or sandalwood oil. Bless it in the name of the Horned God, Lord of the Greenwood. Pass the wand swiftly through the candle flame so that it becomes 'charged' with the power of your Beltane fire. Place the wand upon the dish of earth, saying as you hold it there:

"As the wand is to the earth, so the male is to the female
And the Sun enlivens our blossoming world.
Together they bring joy and bear fruit.
May the God and the Goddess bring forth
(state what it is that you want to manifest)."

Leave the earth and wand upon the altar.

Sit beside the candle flame, allowing yourself to feel peaceful. Gaze into the flame. The next part is different depending on whether you are man or woman.

For a woman: Visualise a red rosebud in your womb. Your womb is the source of your creative power, whether you are a mother or not, you will always birth and create projects, ideas, family. Close your eyes and visualise the light from the candle streaming into your womb so that the rosebud starts to unfold and blossom. As you see this clearly in your mind's eye, be aware that your creative potential is also blossoming.

"I am woman, a daughter of the Goddess, ready to conceive and create, to nurture and tend. I give birth to all that I wish to create. At this time of Beltane, I ask the Horned God to bless me so that I may make manifest (insert the details of what it is that you wish to manifest)."

37

Visualise what it is that you desire, manifesting in your life. See yourself happily and joyfully experiencing the end result of your desires. Open your eyes.

For a Man: Visualise a bright flame burning within your sexual centre, a point at the base of the stomach, just above the pubic hairline. It is your own male strength and energy which may rise through your body to be released as giving, fertilising power, in any form, or may be the potency which impregnates, creating a physical child. It is the force which blesses, and bestows a healing and creative energy, like the shining Sun. Visualise also that you are sitting in a garden and that a rose tree is in front of you, the roses in bud. Say:

"I am man, I am son of the Goddess, and in my passion is beauty, in my warmth is life. I offer my strength and vitality to (insert the details of what it is that you wish to manifest)." Visualise the light streaming from you to a rose upon the tree causing it to unfold, to blossom. Visualise what it is that you desire, manifesting in your life. See yourself happily and joyfully experiencing the end result of your desires. Open your eyes.

(ii) This rite is adapted from the book *Hedge Witch* by Rae Beth, first published by Robert Hale 1990. Includes lines from Rae Beth's original text

Beltane Traditions and Spells

The may, or hawthorn tree, belongs to the time of Beltane and is sacred to the Goddess. On the morning of May 1st, boughs or sprigs of may would be hung from the front door of the house to protect the dwelling against evil spirits. A hawthorn tree standing on its own is said to be a fairy tree, and it would be honoured by tying coloured ribbons from its branches and dancing around it. Wishes were made for good luck in the coming year and offerings of wine or cider were poured into the ground at its roots. It was believed that this would bring a blessing to the crops and also appease the fairies.

On May Day, a May Queen would be chosen, traditionally she would be the fairest maiden in the village, and she would be adorned with beautiful flowers and paraded through the streets. As May Queen, she was allowed to choose a handsome male companion. The May Queen is the representation of the Goddess at Beltane, and her presence at the celebrations was seen as a great blessing.

It is said that any young maiden who ventures out at dawn on May morning and washes her face in the dew will be made beautiful and will find love.

Maypole Magic Spell

Aim: To attract good luck for the coming year.

Tools: A wand or branch, Red and white ribbons, neroli oil.

The most well known Beltane tradition is that of Maypole dancing. A tall pole would be erected and red and white ribbons would be attached from the top of the pole, the colours representing the God and the Goddess. Dancers would then hold the ribbons and weave around each other as they dance around the Maypole, resulting in a beautiful pattern of woven ribbons down the length of the pole. This symbolised the weaving of luck.

To weave your own Maypole spell, take red and white ribbons and wind them around a stick or wand, focussing your wishes and intentions into it as you weave. Anoint the bound wand with neroli oil and state your intentions aloud. Place the ribbon-bound wand upon your altar and every full moon, take it, re-apply the oil and meditate once again upon your wishes. Repeat until they have come to fruition.

Visualisation

Aim: To celebrate and attract passion into your life, to celebrate love and nature.

Tools: Statues or pictures of the Green Lady and the Horned God, two tea lights and holders, green candle, red candle, candlesticks.

Incense: Cedar or sandalwood.

Oil: Cinnamon (for heated passion), cedar or sandalwood.

Offerings: Cake and wine.

Prepare a sacred space as detailed in Chapter One. Light the tea lights in front of the statues or picture. Light the incense. Call upon the Green Lady and the Horned God:

"I call to you, Great Goddess, Green Lady of the Wood, honour us with your presence at this time of Beltane. Great Goddess, imbue us with your passions, your lusty appetites, your love of life. Great Goddess, Green Lady we ask that you be here present at this rite. Hail and welcome!"

"Great Horned God, we call to thee, consort of the Green Lady, bless us with your protective presence, with your strength and blessings. Join with us and the Green Lady, your consort, at this time of passion, of love, lust and merriment. Great Horned God, we bid you hail and welcome!"

Take your offerings and place before the Goddess and God. Say: "Green Lady, Horned God, please accept these offerings of cake and wine, that you may partake of their essence. At this time of frivolity and frolicking, we ask that you bless us with your passion."

Take the green candle and anoint it with cedar or sandalwood oil, ask the Green Lady and Horned God for that which you desire, ask for your heart chakra to be blessed, to be healed, to be open to love. Ask that you may have love in your life that nourishes you and fills you with joy, and also that you may enjoy the love of the Earth. Light your candle from the tea light, say: "So mote it be!" Place your candle in a candlestick.

Take your red candle and/or anoint it with cinnamon oil. Ask the Green Lady and Horned God for passion in love, passion in abundance and fiery passion in your heart. Ask that your base chakra be awakened to the desire of physical love and passion. You can also ask for the physical strength and stamina to match pace with your desires! Light your candle from the tea light and say: "So mote it be!" and place your candle in the candlestick.

Sit back and close your eyes, after making sure that your candles are completely safe. See yourself walking in a beautiful woodland, spring has sprung, and the plants all

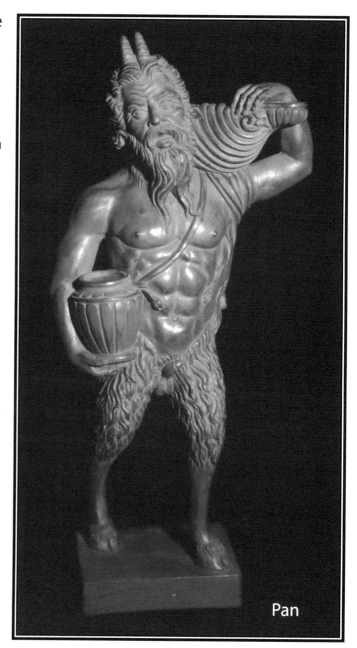

Pan

40

around you are bursting into bud as you walk past. Squirrels dart up the trunk of a tree, chasing each other in playful pursuit. As you near a clearing you hear the call of the stag, echoing through the trees at this time of celebration of nature. A rustling sound from the trees ahead of you gives way to the stag and his doe, emerging into the open, playfully chasing each other. A gentle sound of laughter causes you to look up, and you see them walking toward you from the concealment of the woodland shadows, the Green Lady and her consort, the Horned God. They come towards you, laughing and free spirited, arms entwined around each other in a lovers' embrace. They laugh as the stag turns towards the doe and pursues her back into the wood, their playful chase never ending. The Green Lady and the Horned God ask you what it is that you desire. Is it a new lover? Renewed passion with an existing partner? Perhaps it is self-confidence that you seek? How long it will take? Ask them for their guidance and blessings. What do they say? Perhaps they give you a token gift? If so, what is it? Stay with them awhile, until you are ready to take your leave. As you thank the Green Lady and the Horned God, you turn to leave and a sudden movement on the ground stops you in your tracks. You look down and see two grass snakes entwined in a mating dance, gliding sensuously across your path. After they have passed, you continue on your way, safe in the knowledge that you can return here at any time. Walking towards a lighter area of the wood you find the sunlight streaming down, ever brighter. Walk into the light and through it until you find yourself back in your room once again, seeing yourself sitting in front of your altar. Bring your awareness back into your body and wiggle your toes. In your own time, open your eyes.

Focus on your statues or picture and thank the Green Lady and the Horned God for blessing you with their presence. You may now eat and drink the offerings, in their honour. As you do so, say: "Blessed Be".

Sit awhile and reflect on what you experienced during the visualisation and when you feel ready thank the Green Lady and Horned God for being with you during the ritual and bid them: "Hail and farewell".

Extinguish the tea lights, but let your candles burn all the way down.

Flora

Oh Lady of delight, by the flowers of the field,
And the crops *thy blessings yield*,
Oh Maiden of dew, clear and bright *Daughter of Earth*,
drinking sunlight, Queen of plants, sister of night:
Bring us your grain to *nourish our lives*,
Bring us your fruit wherever it thrives, *Mistress of herbs* unlock your power
And lead us into your leafy bower.
In love and joy we call your name, With comforting hope you ease our pain.
We see thee in the *swelling bud*, We feel thy stirring in our blood;
By leaf and twig, by root and bough, By water and earth, come to us now.[iii]

Flora is the Roman Goddess of Flowers, Gardens, Fertility, Perpetual Youth and the season of Spring. She is the handmaiden of Ceres, the Harvest Goddess, and is represented as a beautiful, alluring nymph, wearing vibrant colours and flowers in her hair. Legend tells us that whenever she shakes her head, she scatters flower petals to the wind. Flora was always honoured as a Goddess of Fruitfulness and Joy, whose blessing brought forth the harvest.

Her festival, the Floralia, was held at the end of April and ran from the 27th for seven days. Women were encouraged to celebrate their beauty and their bodies during this time of merriment, with much drinking and dancing, and all the participants were naked. During the festival beans were scattered to ensure fertility. This continued until the third century AD, when the Roman government decided that all attendees should wear clothes. The festival continued for one more century, until all Pagan festivals were banned. However, remnants of this festival survive today and are to be found within the May Day celebrations. Chariot races were regularly held at the Floralia, and Flora is often called upon by those seeking victory in races. There were theatrical plays, which were often bawdy, and the festival became known for explicit sexual activities. Flora is a very sexy Goddess and is said to have made her fortune as a courtesan. It is also said that many Roman prostitutes called themselves Flora.

It is believed that the Earth was just one colour before Flora. She provided the seeds for mankind to scatter so that they may enjoy the resultant plants and flowers. She loves honey and the bee is her sacred totem. The flowers and plants sacred to Flora are lupin, vetch and wheat flowers, all of which are fertility symbols. During Floralia celebrations, they would be strewn in the streets. Hares and goats were let loose during the chariot races, and these animals were also sacred to Flora.

In Imperial times, Flora's temple in Rome was rededicated on August the 13th. This created a second festival of Flora, which coincided with the ripening of the crops. Her blessings were originally sought during the time of sowing, in order to keep disease off the grain and to ask for a fruitful harvest. This second festival was a time to offer thanks to Flora, as the grain was seen to be flourishing.

Flora's Bath of Beauty

Aim: To appreciate one's own beauty.

Tools: Fresh flower petals, ideally sweet peas, bean blossoms or any seasonal flowers, geranium oil, jasmine oil, rose oil, and lots of candles.

Timing: This spell is best done at the same time as Flora's festival, the Floralia, between April the 27th and May the 3rd.

Fill your bath with as many fresh flower petals as possible, especially sweet peas, lupins, rose

petals, violets. Add two drops each of geranium, jasmine and rose oil. Light candles all around your bathroom. Call upon the Goddess Flora by reciting the invocation on page 43.*(iii)* Get into your bath and soak in the scented water. Meditate upon Flora, Goddess of Beauty and Self-love and as you do, understand that you are also beautiful. After your bath you may also choose to anoint yourself with floral scented oils or lotion. Before you go to sleep, add two more drops each of the oils to your pillow. The following morning take some time after waking and before getting out of bed to bask in the scent of the oils and feel your renewed sense of self esteem.

Visualisation

Aim: To bring love and new beginnings into your life.
Tools: Statue or photo of Flora, pale green and pink candles, candlesticks, rose, geranium, or jasmine oil. You may wish to take a scented floral bath as detailed above.

Create a sacred space as detailed in Chapter One. Place your statue or photo in front of you and call upon the Goddess:

"I call upon thee, Goddess Flora, Lady of Flowers, Be here now and grant us your glorious presence. Oh Lady of Wondrous Beauty, we call to thee at this, your time of festivities. All hail Flora, Goddess of the Floralia! All hail, all hail!"

Anoint the light your green candle with jasmine or geranium oil and ask Flora for the new beginnings that you wish to come into your life. Light the candle and say: "So mote it be!"

Now anoint your pink candle with rose or jasmine oil and ask for love and self-love to blossom and flourish in your life. Light your candle and say: "So mote it be!"

Close your eyes and as you enjoy the scent of the oils, see a beautiful rose arch standing before you, with wild flowers and roses entwined around it and a gossamer veil hanging over the archway, gently rippling in the breeze. See yourself get up and pull aside the veil and walking through into a beautiful garden, full of wild flowers, roses, geraniums, jasmine, sweet peas. All of the beautiful flowers surround you in a vividly abundant display. You walk through this magical

garden until you come to a clearing and there you see her, resplendent and radiant, Flora, the Lady of Flowers. As she steps towards you, you see that everything she touches bursts into flower, even the grass beneath her feet gives way to daisies and buttercups. As she brushes her hand across a vine, it immediately springs forth with abundant grapes emanating a delicate scent. Walk with her awhile, as Flora leads you through her beautiful garden. You stop by

a beautiful water fountain, the water gently splashing and bubbling in the spring sunshine. Floating in the water is a selection of flower buds. As she turns to you, she asks you what it is that you would desire. You tell her, and she invites you to choose one of the buds from the fountain. Select your bud, and as you hold it in your hand, watch in awe as the bud opens up before your eyes, so many petals, so many layers, so many colours, and such a beautiful scent. You hold the beautiful and extraordinary flower in your hand, as Flora touches the exquisite petals gently and tells you about that which is yet to come and how your dreams will come to pass. When you are ready you thank Flora and take your leave of the Goddess, safe in the knowledge that you may return at any time. You make your way back through the garden until you come once again to the rose arch, entwined with wild flowers, with the gossamer veil fluttering gently in the breeze. Pull back the veil once more and step though and see yourself sat before your altar with your candles burning brightly. Bring your awareness back into your body, wiggle your toes and in your own time open your eyes. Thank Flora for her presence and her blessings and bid her: "Hail and farewell!" Let your candles burn all the way down.

48

LITHA - SUMMER SOLSTICE
Amaterasu

"We call to you to you, great *Sun Goddess,*
Who rules the Celestial Plain.
Golden Lady of light and warmth, we welcome you.
Help us when the *storms of life* do frighten us,
Help us to emerge from the darkness and see the
reflection of the Goddess that resides within us all.
Restore us with your *radiant smile.*
Under your reign, all living things rejoice,
Basking in the kiss of your summer power.
We ask for your blessing upon this land
And for all who dwell upon it."

L itha is the ancient name for the time of the Summer Solstice, which is celebrated on June the 21st. Celebrants greet the sun as it rises over the horizon, heralding the dawn of Midsummer's day, the longest day of the year and the shortest night. This celebration honours the sun at the height of its power.

Amaterasu is a Japanese Shinto Sun Goddess, whose name means 'she who shines in the heavens'. In the Shinto pantheon, she is a central character and the eldest daughter of Izanagi. She was born from his left eye as he purified himself in a river. She was so bright and radiant, that her parents sent her up the Celestial Ladder, where she has ruled the Plain of Heaven ever since.

49

Amaterasu had a brother called Susanowa, the God of Storms. He was unpredictable and was always causing trouble, so much so that his father decided to make him God of the Oceans and send him away. But before he left he wanted to say goodbye to his sister. He caused havoc on his journey to meet Amaterasu. Wherever he went he created huge storms and so much noise, that Amaterasu was afraid and ran away to hide. She shut herself in a cave and blocked the entrance with a large boulder.

With Amaterasu's disappearance, the sun had disappeared from the sky, and the world was cast into darkness. Everyone suffered, nothing would grow and demons ruled the Earth.

Despite all their efforts, the other Gods could not persuade Amaterasu to come out of her cave. They asked the Earth spirits to help them, who brought cockerels to crow so that Amaterasu would think that it was morning. They brought beautiful jewels from the mountains and hung them in a tree around in front of the cave, and next to the jewels they hung a mirror. Then a beautiful Goddess called Ama-no-Uzume came to the rescue. She started to dance, a beautiful voluptuous dance, discarding her veils one by one. Faster and faster she danced, until she made the Gods laugh and cry out with delight. The crowd adored her, mesmerised by her dance. They laughed and cheered so much that Amaterasu could hear them from within her cave and she was curious to see what all the fuss was about. Finally, she rolled back the boulder and peered out of her cave. A streak of daylight permeated the darkness, a streak of light, which later became known as the dawn. The Gods saw their chance to restore light to the world and grabbed hold of Amaterasu and pulled her out of the cave. She returned to the sky and light was restored to the world once more.

Then Amaterasu caught sight of her reflection in the mirror that had been hung in the tree by the Earth spirits and she saw how beautiful she was. All of the deities and the Earth spirits gathered around her and told her that the world needed her. She agreed to stay and from that moment the Earth began to warm again, the forest and the fields began to grow once more and the demons were banished. This heralded the beginning of spring.

It is claimed that Amaterasu is directly linked to the lineage of the Imperial Household of Japan and therefore the Emperor and his descendants are said to be descendants of the Goddess herself.

When working magically with Amaterasu, it is possible to restore one's light, one's self esteem. Perhaps your energy levels have been low and you wish to have more vitality. Perhaps your confidence in yourself as an attractive person has taken a knock following the break up of a relationship. Connecting with Amaterasu can help you to bring the energy of the sun back into your life and to restore your belief in yourself. Look into her mirror and see the radiance of the beautiful Goddess smiling back at you, remember who you are and rediscover the beauty within yourself.

Visualisation / Ritual

Aim: To increase vitality and optimism.
Tools: Statue or photo of Amaterasu, orange candle, candlestick, mirror.
Oil: Neroli (orange blossom) or grapefruit.
Incense: Sandalwood.

Create a sacred space as detailed in Chapter One. Light your incense and place it next to your statue or photo of the Goddess. Call upon the Goddess:

"I call to you great Goddess, Amaterasu, Lady of Light, Goddess of the Sun, that gives life to all things on Earth. Be with me now, O Goddess, at this time of Summer Solstice and restore my spirit, imbue me with strength and vitality, as I dance in your beauteous rays may I be filled with laughter and joy. Great Goddess Amaterasu, you who gives life to the land, may you also enliven my endeavours, my loves and my light. May I carry the flame of your light within my heart, to illumine the way ahead. Great Goddess, Amaterasu, I bid you hail and welcome!"

Take your candle and anoint it with neroli or grapefruit oil. Focus upon the candle as you sit in front of your altar and ask for vitality, strength and vigour. Ask for your confidence to shine, to be your true self, for the physical energy and motivation to say what needs to be said and to do what needs to be done. Ask Amaterasu to shine her light in areas of your life that require illumination, that need to flourish and grow. Perhaps a new relationship; to restore your self-confidence; a new job or project. Light the candle and say: "So mote it be!" and place it safely in the candlestick.

Close your eyes and be aware of the candle flame burning in front of you. See yourself walking though a wooded landscape, with the sunlight streaming through the trees. The rays of light are so bright, so golden, as if the trees are alight with the vibrant power of the sun. A figure comes towards you, dancing her solar dance, vibrant with the power of the sun. As she stops before you she extends her hand and asks you to join her in the dance. Together you move and sway, moving swiftly though the trees, the sunlight reflecting from her long tresses. As you stop she turns to you and asks what it is that you desire. Tell her and take note of her answer. She gives you a mirror, take it and look at your reflection. Gaze upon your face and see the warmth and the light of the Goddess smiling back at you. After a while you hand the mirror back to Amaterasu. She tells you what it is that you need to know to enrich your life and help your dreams to become manifest. After a while, she takes your hand once again and leads you towards the golden sun whose rays are streaming through the trees. At the edge of the wood, the sun is so bright, so warm. You take your leave of the Goddess, thanking her, safe in the knowledge that you may return at any time. You walk towards the beautiful light of the sun and walk through it, bathed in its golden rays, feeling its power strengthen and enliven you. Bring your awareness back into your body and wiggle your toes. In your own time open your eyes.

Write down all that Amaterasu said to you and thank the Goddess again. Take the mirror from your altar and spend a few minutes gazing into it, realise that the beauty of the Goddess is now here with you in the material world. Now say:

"Great Amaterasu, Lady of the Sun, I thank you for bestowing your blessings upon me at the time of Summer Solstice. I bid you hail and farewell." Let your candle burn all the way down.

Summer Solstice Mirror Spell

Aim: To draw energy and strength from the sun, that you can carry right through to the Winter Solstice.

Tools: One red candle, one white candle, one small circular mirror, red glass paint or permanent marker, and one tea light candle in a jar.

Timing: The Summer Solstice.

As part of your Solstice celebrations, start this spell indoors the night before the sunrise on the solstice, then complete the spell at sunrise. Light both candles. Using the red glass paint or permanent marker, draw lines on your circular mirror which divide it up equally into eight sections, meeting in the centre. Hold the mirror in your left hand, then cover it with your right and close your eyes. Focus on the image of the flickering candle flames. Visualise the light from the flames coming towards you and entering your body at your solar plexus, then coursing through your body, until it reaches the mirror, which you are holding. Take some rest and rise again before dawn. Just before sunrise, go outside and light the tea light just as the sun rises. Place the mirror before you and as the light of the sun illuminates the mirror, raise your arms up towards the sun and say:

"Great Sun, source of power and strength, light the fire within me that I maybe strong and invigorated with your sacred fire. Grant me the energy to sustain me until the time of Winter Solstice".

Keep your mirror and use it daily until the Winter Solstice. Each time you look into it, remember that the Goddess and the power of the Sun are reflected back at you.

Summer Solstice Love Spell

Aim: To bring love into your life.

Tools: Yellow cloth, gold candle in a candlestick, summer blossoms, red rose petals, rose oil.

Crystals: Rose quartz, crystal quartz, citrine, jade (or another green stone), red jasper, small bag or pouch.

This ritual may be done indoors, but is best done outdoors if possible. Take a purifying bath before doing the ritual. Add flowers and scented rose oil. Cleanse your crystals in the bath water.

Create a sacred space as detailed in Chapter One. Make an altar with a yellow cloth to represent the sun at its height and place some summer blossoms upon it. Place the gold candle centrally on your altar. Sprinkle the red rose petals all around the candle. Place the rose quartz in front of the candle and arrange the remaining crystals around it.

Hold the crystal quartz and say:

"May love be pure and shine brightly."

Put the quartz back and hold the citrine and say:

"May love be as joyful as a summer's day."

Put the citrine back and hold the jade and say:

"May love grow as the green plants in summer."

Put the jade back and hold the jasper and say:

"May love burn like an ardent fire."

Put the jasper back and hold the rose quartz and say:

"I love and am worthy of love. May I attract the right kind of love for me, happy, fruitful and fulfilling."

Hold the rose quartz against your heart and feel love filling your whole being. Gather all the stones with a few rose petals in both hands. Whilst holding them, say:

"Bring love to my heart, that I may love and be loved in perfect harmony."

Shake the stones three times and put them and a few rose petals in the bag. Hold the stones in your hands at any time to reinforce the spell.

Sekhmet

"O star of the lion's heart, I *behold thee* in the *heavens*,
Embolden my heart, O Sekhmet, Embolden my soul, O flame, O *lion star*.
Send forth thy power as I raise my sword on high.
Thou *star of Sekhmet*, kindle my sword with *thy flame*.
Let it shine with the light of thy red dawn.
O star of the *lion Goddess*, shine thou upon my path
Shine thou upon me, for I am true unto the Goddess.
Shine thou upon my sword for *I am true unto Sekhmet*
Shine thou upon my way for I am true to thee." [i]

Sekhmet is one of the oldest of the Egyptian deities. Her name originates from the word 'Sekhem' which means power and as a result Sekhmet's name is often translated as 'Powerful One'. She is shown as a woman with the head of a lioness and she often has the sun disc upon her head.

As she is closely linked with the sun, Sekhmet represents the heat of the midday sun, intense and fierce. She was also known as the Goddess of War and her ferocity was terrifying, as was her roar. Her strength and her power were thought to be able to avert plague and cure disease and hence she became the patron Goddess of Surgeons in Egypt and was known as the 'Bone-setter'.

The 'Lady of Terror' also became known as the 'Lady of Life', which is why she is often shown holding the Ankh, a symbol of life. So Sekhmet became known as both a destructive and a creative force.

According to the myth, the Sun God Ra became very angry with mankind because they were not abiding by his laws, so he decided to punish them. He sent his daughter, Sekhmet, to punish and slay them. She rampaged across the Earth, wreaking havoc and killing everyone in her path. The fields were awash with human blood as she went about her task. However, Ra was not cruel by nature and he started to regret this course of action, after all, if Sekhmet slaughtered everyone on the Earth, there would be no one left to worship him and he didn't want that. He asked Sekhmet to stop, but she would not listen, she was so intent upon completing her task. The taste of blood was fresh in her mouth and she would not stop until every human being was dead. So something needed to be done. Ra took seven thousand jugs of beer and mixed them with pomegranate juice. The mixture was the colour of blood and he left it where Sekhmet would find it. She drank greedily of the 'blood' and became so drunk that she slept for three whole days. By the time she woke up, her desire for blood had waned and she was probably a little hungover. She forgot about her need to wipe out every human being upon the Earth and so humanity was saved. The first thing that Sekhmet saw when she awoke was Ptah, the patron God of Sculptors, Builders and Craftsmen. Sekhmet immediately fell in love with him and they were together from that time on.

When working with Sekhmet you can ask for the strength and the confidence to stand up for yourself. Perhaps you have felt overshadowed at work, or even bullied. Perhaps you feel unconfident about presenting yourself in a job interview or in social situations. Perhaps you fear confrontation and always feel defeated by anyone who opposes you. By working with Sekhmet, you can reassert your own self-confidence, become stronger mentally, face challenges without fear and speak up for yourself. Sometimes this may take a 'destructive' form if things need to be removed from your life. Or it may manifest as a 'creative' force as you ask for the confidence to become who you are meant to be and fulfil your true potential.

Visualisation /Ritual

Aim: To increase confidence, to stand up for yourself, to face an enemy or opposition.
Tools: Statue or photo of Sekhmet, red and orange candle, candlesticks.
Oils: Sandalwood.
Incense: Sandalwood.
Offerings: Stargazer or oriental scented lilies, beer mixed with pomegranate juice.

Create a sacred space as detailed in Chapter One. Light your incense and place your offerings upon the altar. Call upon the Goddess:

"I call to thee, O great Goddess Sekhmet, Lady of the Flame and lioness headed Goddess of Egypt. Be with me, O Sekhmet, that I may receive the blessing of your strength, your power and your healing. Please accept these offerings of incense, flowers and blood red beer. Great Goddess Sekhmet, who prowls the deserts of Egypt, I bid you Hail and Welcome!"

Close your eyes and imagine Sekhmet walking towards you and entering into your photo / statue. Open your eyes after a while, and take your red candle and anoint it with sandalwood oil. Focus upon the candle and face your image of the Goddess. Say aloud that which you would desire, especially all matters to do with physical strength, passion, the ability to stand tall and proud, the courage to face your fears, to face bullies. Ask for Sekhmet's help in certain situations that you find difficult and unnerving. Light your candle and place it in the candlestick in front of your statue / photo on the left, and say: "So mote it be!"

Take your orange candle and anoint it with sandalwood oil, then focus your intentions into the candle. Ask Sekhmet for help with self-confidence, for the ability to shine, to be the best that you can be, for help with all communications and negotiations. Light your candle, say: "So mote it be!" and place it in the candlestick before the Goddess on the right of her. Close your eyes and visualise the two flickering flames of your candles, burning each side of her image. In your mind's eye, see yourself walking across a desert landscape towards a temple. At the entrance you see two stone pillars, with flaming torches at the top, the flames burning brightly and the flames reaching higher and higher. Make your way towards two pillars of flames and walk through them into the central courtyard of the temple, the inner sanctum. Here you see her, standing tall, with such prowess as befits the Lion Queen of the Desert. She moves with grace and elegance as she approaches you. Her power and radiance illuminate your spirit. She reaches out her hand and you see that she holds an Ankh towards you, the symbol of life. Take it in your hand and feel the strength and vitality streaming into you through your fingers. You now feel enlivened and empowered, and able to meet your challenges head on. Sekhmet gives you a message, which will help you to proceed onwards in your situation, with confidence and power. She then invites you to drink from her chalice, a red intoxicating beer, sweetened with the juice of pomegranates. When you feel ready, thank the Goddess for her help and her blessings and take your leave of the temple, safe in the knowledge that you can return here at any time. As you walk through the two flaming pillars that guard the temple entrance, you find yourself once again back in your room, with the altar before you, illuminated by the two flickering flames of your candles. Bring your awareness back into your body and open your eyes. Write down that which Sekhmet told you and then thank her once again for her presence during this rite. You may now bid her: "Hail and farewell!" Let your candles burn all the way down.

Sekhmet's Casket

Aim: To contain anger and negativity.
Tools: Photo or statue of Sekhmet, sandalwood incense, a small box or casket, red paint, red candle, candlestick, paper, pen.

Sekhmet's casket is a container to hold all your rage, anger, and negativity. In this ritual, you can hand all of these emotions over to Sekhmet so that she can take them away and turn the energy in to something more positive for you.

Create a sacred space as detailed in Chapter One. Light the incense and call upon the Goddess Sekhmet:

"Great Goddess Sekhmet, of Fire and Wrath, bestow upon me your fiery blessing, that I may release my anger and pain, transform my wrath and my ire into that of constructive force. I

call to thee, O Sekhmet, attend this rite and grant your power to me this night. Great Goddess Sekhmet, I bid you hail and welcome."

Find a container with a lid or opening and paint it with a bright red paint. As you apply it, imagine all your rage pouring into the paint. Leave it to dry. Light a red candle, and write down everything which you are angry and upset about. Fold the paper and place it into the casket. Meditate on the flame of the red candle and visualise all of the negative things burning away from your life. Then remove the folded paper from the casket and burn it in the flame of the candle, saying:

"I hereby release all that no longer serves me. May all of this anger, frustration and fear be gone from my life. So mote it be!" Let the candle burn all the way down.

Healing Anger

Aim: To transform your anger into a more positive force.
Tools: Red candles, a cup of red wine or pomegranate juice mixed with beer.
Preparation: Wear something red.

Create a sacred space as detailed in Chapter One. Then sit facing the South, light your red candle, and call upon the great Goddess Sekhmet:

"Great Goddess, Sekhmet, Lady of the Flame, I call to thee to attend this rite, aid me in thy work that I may transform my anger into a greater force. Please accept this offering in your honour Great Sekhmet, I bid you hail and welcome!"

Place the wine or pomegranate juice mixed with beer on the altar. Close your eyes and imagine Sekhmet sitting before you, calm and listening, with the Ankh symbol in her hand. Think about what is making you angry and when you fell ready say it out loud, say it to Sekhmet:

"I am angry about......... (Detail what it is that has angered you)." Let yourself feel the full range of emotions with your anger, perhaps frustration, upset, betrayal. Send all of these emotions to Sekhmet. After a while you feel a golden stream of light and energy coming back towards you, you feel it in your solar plexus, your centre, you feel it in your heart, your mind. When you are done, thank Sekhmet for being present and bid her: "Hail and farewell!"

Let your candle burn all the way down.

A Prayer to Sekhmet for Protection Against Harm
Originally composed as a protection heka (spell) for an American soldier serving in Iraq.

Lady of the *Burning Sands*,

Sekhmet, Mistress of Terror!

May no enemy find me,

May no harm approach me,

Your **sacred fire** surrounds me,

No evil can withstand *Your Eye*. [iii]

LAMMAS

Gaia

O Goddess Earth, you are the source of all that nurtures our essence, our life force.
O gracious mother, your *fertile* powers produce
an *abundance* of fruits and flowers.
All-flowery dæmon, centre of the world, around thy orb,
the beauteous stars are hurled with rapid whirl, *eternal and divine*.
Through starry skies your skill and *wisdom shine*.
Come, *blessed Goddess*, and increase the fruits of thy constant care. *(i)*

Lammas is a Celtic fire festival and traditionally marked the start of the harvest. It is also known as Lughnasadh, which is the Irish festival to honour the Sun God, Lugh. It is a time to give thanks to the Goddesses for that which you have, and to reap what you have sown during the preceding year.

Gaia is a Greek Goddess who cares for the Earth. She was a very early Earth Goddess and according to myth, she was born from Chaos, the great void of emptiness in the universe. She is depicted surrounded by the stars and holding the Earth gently in her hands, but also as a matronly woman who has half her body embedded within the ground, to show that she is 'of the earth'. She sometimes also appears as a woman reclining upon the Earth surrounded by a host of Carpi, who are the infant Gods of the Fruits of the Earth. In Greece, Gaia was seen as the original Goddess from which all the other Gods and Goddesses originated. Her sacred animals are the serpent, the lunar bull, the pig, and bees.

Many Pagans actively worship Gaia, and share a range of beliefs as to her true nature. Some believe that Gaia is the Earth whilst others see her as a Goddess of the Earth. Many see Gaia as the Goddess of all Creation, the original Mother Goddess who gave birth to all other Gods and Goddesses. Therefore, she is often believed to be greater than the Earth, encompassing the whole universe.

Gaia is believed to be the Goddess who originally ruled the famous oracle of Delphi, although it was later associated with Themis, and later still Apollo. The oracle was given by a priestess called Pythia, who would go into a trance after inhaling the fumes of pungent herbs. Whilst in trance, she would become the voice of the Goddess and give spiritual insight and wisdom to the visitors. The fact that it was a priestess, not a priest who presided over the sanctuary at Delphi, indicates that it is more likely to have been first dedicated to a Goddess, not a God. In Ancient Greece an oath sworn in the name of Gaia was considered the most binding of all.

Gaia gave birth to Uranus, the starry sky, so that he might cover her. She then went on to have many children with him, including the Titans, the Cyclops, and the spirits of punishment known as the Erinyes. Gaia was fearful for the safety of her children as Uranus feared their strength over him, so she hid them all within herself. However, she found her offspring very uncomfortable and it was sometimes painful to keep them all within her. She enlisted the help of her youngest son Cronos and asked him to castrate Uranus. This would sever the union between the Earth and Sky, and prevent Gaia and Uranus having any more children. Gaia gave Cronos a small flint sickle to use as a weapon. He hid and waited until Uranus came to Gaia to make love to her. Cronos picked his moment and leapt forward as Uranus drew near, castrating his father with the sharp flint sickle. The drops of blood that bled from the wound fell to Earth and as they did, the Erinyes (the Furies) were born. His testicles fell into the sea and brought forth the Goddess of Love and Sexual Pleasure, Aphrodite.

Working with Gaia can help you in all areas of healing. She is especially helpful when it comes to grounding yourself. Ask her to share her abundance with you, that you may freely enjoy the fruits of the Earth and that your Earthly needs be met.

Mother Earth, renew and restore my
knowledge and *respect* for you.
As my awareness of you as a living being grows,
Cultivate the knowledge that *I am part of you*
and you are part of me." [(ii)]

Gaia Healing Spell

Aim: To send healing to the planet.
Tools: Work outside in the woods or garden, use branches or stones to form a circle around you at least 4 inches in diameter. Pale blue candle and candlestick, lavender oil.
Incense: Cedar.

Kneel in the centre of the circle. Light the incense, and anoint the light blue candle with lavender oil. Focus your intention into the candle and say:

"Goddess of the Stars, I call to you,
that you may bestow your blessings upon this planet Earth.
Gaia, may your power grow strong again,
Let the Earth be whole again,
Let the healing power begin.
By earth, by air, by fire, by water
Receive this prayer from me, your daughter/son"

Light the candle, say: "So mote it be!" and place the candle in the candlestick. Let the candle burn all the way down.

Release of Pain Spell

Aim: To heal pain, emotional or physical.

This is to be done on a rainy night outdoors. Stand in the rain and let it touch you, let yourself get wet. When the rainfall is very heavy recite the incantation and make sure that you say the words with power and conviction. Let the spell come from the heart, becoming louder as you chant:

"Rain, rain, wash away the pain,
Rain, rain, release the pain,
Never to return again,
Rain, rain, wash away the pain,
Rain, rain, release the pain,
Never to return again.
Cry for me, take away my tears,
Cry for me, take away my fears,
Restore my health, my strength do gain!
Restore my health, my strength do gain!
Restore my health, my strength do gain!
Restore my health, my strength do gain!"

Hold your hands up to the sky and let the rain fill your palms. Wash your face and eyes with it and say:

"Let the tears wash all pain away, that it may be taken deep into the ground beneath your feet. I release all pain and negativity – NOW! So mote it be!"

Imagine the pain washing away, leaving your body and entering the earth.

Visualisation / Ritual

Aim: To bring about healing and resolution to disputes. To send healing to a person or a situation. To send healing to the Earth.

Tools: Statue or photo of Gaia. Plant pot, earth, pen and paper, pale green candle, rosemary or sage oil.

Incense: Sage or cedar.

Create a sacred space as detailed in Chapter One. Light the incense in front of your image of Gaia. Call upon the Goddess:

"Great Goddess Gaia, I call to you, who holds the Earth in your hands and imbues your healing upon it and within it. Great Gaia, I call upon you, Mother Earth, be here now at this rite in your honour and bless me with your presence, that I may be healed with your love and your power. Great Goddess Gaia, I bid you hail and welcome!"

Anoint your candle with rosemary or sage oil and ask Gaia for her help to heal or solve the problem. Ask for her healing to be sent to that person or situation and that reconciliation and healing can take place. Light your candle and say: "So mote it be!"

Close your eyes and imagine yourself walking across the hills and dales of the English countryside under the light of the moon. As you walk across a beautiful lush field, you see and sense a movement around you. A beautiful Goddess emerges from the field, as if she had arisen from the very ground itself. She rises up and as she stands before you, illuminated by the moon and the stars, you see the sparkling lights of the stars reflected upon her flowing robes. She takes you by the hand and ascends into the night sky. Light as a feather, you rise up alongside her, soaring high above the fields, the hills and dales. Higher and higher you both fly until you find yourself in the realms of the stars and moon. Gaia brings you both gently to stop and you are suspended in the night sky. A beautiful nebula illuminates the sky around you, vibrant with glorious shades of green and blue. Gaia reaches out her hands and picks up a globe. As she shows it to you, you see that this is the Earth, as small as a ball in her hands. She asks you to put your hands upon the Earth and to share with her the healing magic that she shall impart. As you do so, you feel the pulsating energy coming from her hands and entering the Earth, and you think upon your problem or the person who requires healing and or send healing to the Earth. See the problem from a new perspective and understand that as you do, healing will applied to the situation and that the healing may take another form other than that which you envisage, for all healing is good for those involved. Stay a while with your hands upon the Earth and see what images or information come to you. What does Gaia say to you about your problem? After a while, she places the Earth back and takes your hand once again. Gently, you descend through the starry night sky until once again you can see the hills and dales beneath you. Gaia guides you gently back to the Earth and you feel your feet touch the ground once more. She releases your hand and bids you goodbye, for now. You thank her for her blessings, safe in the knowledge that you can visit her again whenever you wish. She turns and walks away across the field and as you watch her go, she becomes absorbed by the Earth. Become aware of your altar in your room with the pale green candle burning brightly before Gaia's image.

Bring your awareness back into your body and wiggle your toes. Open your eyes in your own time. Think on what Gaia has told you and write it down. Place the paper in a small pot filled with earth and cover it with more earth. When you feel ready or your wishes have become manifest, bury the earth and paper outside in the garden or woods. Thank the Goddess for joining you this night and bid her: "Hail and farewell." Let your candles burn all the way down.

Ceres - Demeter

O Goddess Earth, you are the source of all that nurtures our essence, our life force.
O gracious mother, your *fertile* powers produce
an *abundance* of fruits and flowers.
All-flowery dæmon, centre of the world, around thy orb,
the beauteous stars are hurled with rapid whirl, *eternal and divine*.
Through starry skies your skill and *wisdom shine*.
Come, *blessed Goddess*, and increase the fruits of thy constant care. *(i)*

Ceres is a Roman Goddess of Agriculture, identified with the Greek Goddess Demeter, who rules over crops, the fertility of the land as well as motherly relationships. She is the Goddess attributed with the discovery of spelt wheat, the yoking of oxen and ploughing, the sowing, protection and nourishing of the young seed, and the gift of agriculture to humankind. Before Ceres gifted these skills to humanity it is believed that man survived on nothing but acorns. Ancient man was believed to be nomadic and without any organised settlements or law governing society. Ceres was the first Goddess to 'break open the Earth' and enable man to bring forth the fruits of the Earth, and subsequently, her festivals mark the most important times and activities of the agricultural year. She has the power to fertilise and multiply all seeds, whether they be plant or animal. Therefore it was believed that all animal offspring and new crops belonged to the Goddess. In about 500 BC there was a famine in Rome. After consulting the Sybilline Books (a collection of ancient prophecies), it was decided to build a temple to Ceres on the Aventine Hill. This was dedicated in 493 BC. Priestesses were always brought from southern Italy, and the prayers were said in Greek. This temple also functioned as a depository for historical archives, and became a centre for the distribution of food to the poor. In January, Ceres was appeased with offerings of spelt wheat and a pregnant sow at a festival called 'Feriae Sementivae', which was always held just before the sowing season. In Ancient Rome they would also celebrate Ceres with a festival in mid to late April lasting seven days, which was called Cerealia. There would be games to entertain the people and they commenced with a horse race in the Circus Maximus, whose starting point lay just below the Aventine Temple of Ceres. A ritual followed the race, held at night, whereby flaming torches would be tied to the tails of live foxes and they would be released into the Circus. Whilst the original purpose of this ritual is not known, it may have been intended to ritually cleanse the growing crops and to protect them from disease and vermin. Ceres was also honoured at the time of the harvest as the Goddess of the Crops and the modern word 'cereal' is derived from her name. As well as ruling over her agricultural domain, she was also revered as a Mother Goddess and governed all areas to do with fertility.

Ceres is also closely identified with the Greek Goddess Demeter. At the heart of the myth of Demeter is her relationship with her daughter, Persephone (see chapter on Imbolc). Persephone became the consort of Hades, God of the Underworld, also known as Pluto in Roman mythology.

As well as being the Goddess of the Harvest, Demeter also controlled the seasons. When she was living happily with Persephone, the Earth was abundant and perpetual summer, but after her disappearance, her despair caused the crops to die. So, as well as being a Goddess that could bring life, she also held the power to destroy it. Her grief brought about the decimation of the Earth as all crops withered and died. Finally, Zeus was forced to intervene and arrange for Persephone's return from the Underworld. Hades agreed, but said he would release Persephone only on the condition that she hadn't eaten any food during her stay in the Underworld. But before Persephone was released, she ate six pomegranate seeds, which led to her annual return to the Underworld for six months of the year. This time became known as the reason for the changes in the seasons, as when Persephone descended in autumn, her mother Demeter would cause the crops to stop growing until her return in spring.

You can work with Demeter if you have difficulties with your own mother / daughter relationships, perhaps to seek greater understanding of each other or to heal a rift. You may choose to work with both Persephone and Demeter at the same time, thereby bringing forth the guidance of both Goddesses.

When working with Ceres, you can ask for a good harvest in your life, in your endeavours. "As you sow, so shall you reap" is a wise old adage, which is very appropriate when working with this Goddess. You may wish to work with the Wheel of the Year, asking for Ceres's blessing on your endeavours in January before you 'sow the seeds' of your future projects. Ask for her continued blessings in April, to help protect and nurture the growth of your projects and celebrate her at Lammas, at harvest time when you shall reap the rewards of your endeavours.

Harvest Ritual / Visualisation

Aim: To reap the rewards of your endeavours.
Tools: Statue or photo of Demeter or Ceres, green candle, candlestick, cauldron, a plate of bread, a chalice of wine, and leaves and flowers for decoration upon the altar.
Incense: Cedar or another woody scent.

Create a sacred space as detailed in Chapter One. Light the incense and place it before your image of Demeter or Ceres. Call upon the Goddess:

" We call to you great Mother of the Harvest, Demeter / Ceres, Goddess of the Corn, bless us with your presence at this time of Lammas and help us to reap the rewards of that which we have sown. Bless us with the abundant cornucopia that you cradle in your

arms and nourish us with the fruits of our labours. Great Goddess Demeter/Ceres, we bid you hail and welcome!"

Close your eyes and visualise Demeter or Ceres coming towards you and entering into the statue or photo upon your altar.

Open your eyes once more and take your candle. Light the candle and place it in the cauldron and say:

"This candle represents the harvest within my life. All of the goals I have worked on this year are now nearing completion. I receive the harvest of others who work to my good, and reject any harvest of any who would work against me. I prepare myself in body, mind, and soul, for the time of winter and rest."

Set the chalice of wine in front of your image of the Goddess and say:

"Great Goddess Demeter / Ceres, please accept this offering of wine, made from the fruits of thine Earth."

Place the bread before the Goddess and say:

"I offer you this bread, great Goddess, which is made of the grain from your bountiful fields that nourishes us so that we may grow strong."

Close your eyes and see yourself walking across a beautiful field of golden wheat, with the glowing evening sun setting in the sky before you. You see a figure walking towards you, at first it is hard to see her clearly as the sun is behind her and surrounds her with a beautiful golden glow. As she comes closer to you, you see her in all her resplendent glory, dressed in flowing robes of russet and gold, cradling a cornucopia in her arms, overflowing with the abundant fruits of nature. Ask her that which you would desire, what it is that you wish to harvest in your life, which dreams you wish to bring to reality. She is the Mother Goddess and also the mother of a daughter. Perhaps you wish to speak to her as if to your mother, perhaps to resolve misunderstandings, or to ask for guidance. Walk with her awhile, through the golden fields of ripened wheat. Listen to her guidance. As you reach the edge of the field, she stops and asks you to choose from the fruits of her cornucopia. What is it that you pick? Eat of the fruit and feel the nourishment flowing into you as you eat, strengthening you, enlivening you and filling you with joy. When you feel ready, you thank the Goddess for her bountiful blessings and take your leave of her, safe in the knowledge that you may return at any time. You walk towards the golden sun, sitting low in the sky and as you become bathed in its light you find your self back in

Priestesses of Avalon tending
the Lammas fire

Preparing to face the fire

your room once again, and see yourself sat in front of your altar. Bring your awareness back into your body and wiggle your toes. In your own time, open your eyes. Take the bread and eat some of it and drink some of the wine. As you do so, say: "Hail Demeter, hail Ceres!"

Thank the Goddess for being present at the rite and bid her: "Hail and farewell!" Let your candle burn all the way down. Take the remaining bread and wine and throw it out into the garden or woods as an offering to the animals.

Each Lammas, in Glastonbury a large event is held called the Goddess Conference, where women gather from around the world and celebrate the Goddesses. To honour this ancient fire festival, they host a Lammas fire ceremony each year. In 2009 the ceremony took the form of a fire walking ritual. Three fires were lit, one to represent the Maiden, the Mother and the Crone. The drummers came forth and drummed in the fire and Priestesses gathered round, waiting for the flames to subside and the embers to glow. Finally, as night fell, the fires were ready and one by one, the people gathered around the fire to face their fears. Summoning their courage, they walked barefoot across the hot coals, making their wishes and affirmations as they strode forth.

Spell for the Mother

Aim: To heal a rift with your mother, to ask for help from the Mother Goddess, to ask for guidance in a mother and daughter relationship.

Tools: Statue or photo of Demeter and Persephone, tea light and holder, pale blue candle, yellow candle, candlesticks, a photo of your mother or daughter (if your query is related to your them). lavender oil, and geranium oil.

Create a sacred space as detailed in Chapter One. Light the tea light and place it in front of the image of the Goddess on your altar. Call upon the Goddess in her Mother aspect:

"Great Mother Goddess Demeter, I call to you, mother of a daughter, mother of mine. I ask that you be here now at this rite, to join with me and aid me in my quest. Great Goddess Demeter, I bid you hail and welcome. Great daughter Goddess, Persephone, daughter of Demeter, I call to you to join me at the rite for greater understanding of my plight. I bid you hail and welcome!" Close your eyes and visualise the Goddesses coming towards you and entering into the statue or photo. Open your eyes.

Say aloud what it is that troubles you, what it is that you need help with and ask for Demeter's and Persephone's help and guidance in resolving it and finding a way to move forward. Take your pale blue candle and anoint it with lavender oil, ask for healing for yourself and your mother or daughter, healing of the mind the emotions and the soul, healing of the situation that you find yourself in. Light your candle from the tea light before the Goddess, say: "So mote it be!" and place it in a candlestick. Now take your yellow candle and anoint it with geranium oil. Ask for balance and tolerance in communications, for each person to understand the other's point of view, for a peaceful resolution to be found. Light your candle from the tea light and say: "So mote it be!"

Close your eyes and imagine yourself talking with the Goddesses, telling them about your concerns and the situation that is troubling you. Listen carefully to their advice. Now imagine yourself having a peaceful and productive conversation with your mother or daughter and that solutions are being found, with understanding and healing taking the place of misunderstanding, argument and regret. See everyone smiling, secure in the knowledge that they have been heard, that they have been understood.

Bring your awareness back into the room once again and open your eyes. Thank the Goddesses for their presence and their valuable guidance and bid them: "Hail and farewell!" Let your candles burn all the way down.

The Maiden and Mother fires are finely ready for us

MABON - AUTUMN EQUINOX

Themis

By Gareth Medway

Illustrious Themis, of *celestial birth*, thee I invoke,
young blossom of the Earth. Beauteous-eyed virgin,
first from thee alone *prophetic oracles* to men were known,
given from the deep recesses of the fane in sacred Pytho, where renowned you reign.
Honoured by all, of form divinely bright, *majestic virgin*,
wandering in the night mankind from thee first learnt initial rites,
and *Bacchus's* nightly choirs thy soul delights.[i]

Mabon is the ancient name for the time of the Autumn Equinox and the name is derived from 'Mabon ap Modron', which is Welsh and means Great Son of the Great Mother. It is the time when the harvest should have been completed and the spirit of the Great Son is believed to be present in the newly harvested crops of Mother Earth.

Themis is often thought of as the Goddess of Justice, however as we look more closely at her story we discover that there is so much more to her than that. She is the daughter of Uranus, God of Heaven, and Gaia, Goddess of the Earth. She was married to Zeus, King of the Gods, and they had three daughters, Eunomia, Goddess of Harmony, Dike, Goddess of Justice, and Eirene, Goddess of Peace. Zeus later divorced her, but she continued to convene the assemblies of the Gods on Olympus.

It has been declared that the laws of physics are all that is necessary to explain the universe and its origins in the Big Bang. This raises the question, where did the laws of physics come from? Themis is described as the Goddess of Balance, and hence the laws of physics originated from her.

Themis presided over the oracles, which were regularly consulted by the Greeks. In Ancient Greece, many people would consult the oracles by visiting a temple of a particular Goddess or God and receive 'channelled' messages from the Priestess, who was believed to be quoting the voice of the Goddess or God.

Legend has it that the world was once destroyed in a tremendous flood, of which the only survivors were an elderly couple named Deucalion and Pyrrha, who took refuge in a small boat, which eventually deposited them at the top of Mount Parnassus. After the waters receded, they walked down until they came to a temple of Themis, now despoiled with seaweed. They decided to enter and to seek guidance from the oracle. Normally the oracles would be given by a Priestess, but of course there were now none. Yet, when they entered, and asked aloud how the world could be repopulated, the voice of the Goddess herself spoke to them, and said: "Depart from the temple, cover your heads, loosen the girdles of your garments, and throw the bones of your Great Mother behind you." After a pause, Pyrrha said that she would not do that, lest her mother's spirit be disturbed thereby. But Deucalion said that Themis would not order them to commit desecration, and that her words must have a symbolic significance. After they had considered this further, he finally realised that their 'Great Mother' meant Mother Earth, not a person, and that her bones were in fact stones. So they left the temple, went down the hillside, covered their heads, loosened their girdles, and threw stones behind them. As they landed, miraculously they began to lose their hardness, and as they softened they grew, and their shapes turned into a semblance of humans. Finally, they came to life, and were new people. Those thrown by Deucalion metamorphosed into men, while those thrown by Pyrrha became women. And so a new human race came about.

This fable illustrated the importance of the oracles to the ancients, who consulted them as the modern people consult tarot readers, psychics and astrologers. When Alyattes, the King of Lydia, fell ill, he sent messengers to the oracle at Delphi, which was presided over by Themis. The Priestess ordered him to rebuild the temple of Athena, which had been accidentally destroyed by fire. He built two temples to Athena, and recovered his health. His son Croesus decided to test this oracle, and sent emissaries to inquire what he would do on a prearranged day. The Priestess answered in verse:

"I know the number of the sands, and measure out the sea,
And understand the dumb, and hear those who speak not.
There comes to my senses the scent of a hard-shelled tortoise
Boiling in bronze, with it is the flesh of a lamb,
Bronze is the cauldron, and bronze is its lid."

In fact, Croesus, on the day in question, had cut up a tortoise and a lamb and boiled them together in a bronze cauldron with a bronze lid. He was amazed as he could not fathom how anyone would be able to guess this. So from this time forth, he always took the Delphic oracle seriously. In modern times, this would be called 'validation' during a psychic reading, whereby the reader tells the querent some detailed information that they could not possibly have known.

The symbols of Themis are the lamp, the comb, and the herb marjoram, but more particularly the scales and the sword, although these two have also come to be particularly associated with her daughter, Dike, Goddess of Justice, who was called Astraea by the Romans. Her statue, brandishing these implements, is placed above the Old Bailey Courts of Law. A cynical legend states that in very ancient times, when the Silver Age gave way to the Bronze Age, Astraea left the Earth in disgust and went to live among the stars as the constellation Virgo.

These foregoing apparently disparate associations to the Goddess are, in fact, closely linked. Themis is the personification of the laws of physics, which arise naturally from the union of Heaven and Earth, that is to say Spirit and Matter. Her scales symbolise the fact that Nature is perfectly balanced in her reactions.

These laws do not merely govern the present, but indicate what will come to pass in the future, because of what the Indians term 'karma', that your actions, good or bad, will return to you sooner or later. Thus, the inspired oracles can foretell what is to come. The name of Themis is related to the English word 'doom', which is usually regarded as a fearful word, because most people think that the retribution to come to them will be terrible.

People are generally reluctant to wait for a 'doom' to return, which may take many years or even lifetimes, hence they pass laws and punish those who transgress them. Earthly justice is an attempt to emulate cosmic justice, although this being an imperfect world, it can go wrong. The balance of Themis is also capable, in principle, of bringing Peace and Harmony to the world.

Modern astronomers have given the name to the twenty-fourth asteroid that was discovered, which is accordingly known as 24-Themis. Recently, they discovered that it is covered with water and ice, raising the possibility that it could be home to primitive life. This in turn may shed light on the theory that the earliest life arose on the asteroids, and was brought to Earth when an asteroid crashed here.

Themis is associated with the Autumn Equinox because, firstly, it is one of the two times of the year when light and dark are exactly balanced. Moreover, it is the moment when the Sun moves from Virgo, the sign of her daughter Astraea, to Libra, the sign of her symbol the scales. Also it is around the time of the harvest, that is, the time when what you have given out returns to you.

Justice Spell

Aim: To achieve Justice in a situation that is troubling you.

Tools: Statue or photo of Themis, old fashioned style scales (not digital!), a sword (a paperknife will do), a lamp or lantern with a candle in, a comb, and the herb marjoram. Also, you can add a shell and a crystal, ideally an amethyst, but any stone of the quartz family will suffice. For this particular ritual, some fruit such as apples or grapes, a blue candle, cedar incense. If you cannot obtain all of her symbols, don't worry, some will suffice as many are used to simply dress the altar.

Create a sacred space as detailed in Chapter One. Light the incense and place it by the photo or statue of Themis. Call upon the Goddess, say: "Almighty Themis, daughter of Heaven and Earth, ruler of the cosmic balance, and your beautiful daughter Dike, also known as Astraea, hear my call to thee: (explain the circumstances in which you have been treated unjustly)." Finish with: "May justice be done."

Eat some of the fruit and say: "As the fruit, is the consequence of the planting and the nurturing, so may I receive what I deserve."

End with simple a feast of bread. (Caution: this will only work if you really are in the right!)

Spell to Bring Harmony into Your Home

Create a sacred space as detailed in Chapter One. Set up the altar as above, with in addition a little salt, a small dish of water, candle, frankincense incense, and a bell. Also required is an 'sprinkler', which could be a sprig of heather or other plant with small leaves and say:

"Almighty Themis, daughter of Heaven and Earth, ruler of the cosmic balance, and your delightful daughter Eunomia, bring harmony into this home, that it may be a place of joy and happiness."

86

Say over the salt: "Blessed be this creature of Earth, in the names of Themis and Eunomia." Then say over the water: "Blessed be this creature of Water, in the names of Themis and Eunomia." Add the salt to the water. Carry the dish around your home, using the 'sprinkler' to sprinkle droplets all around, taking care around electrical appliances!

Light the candle and say: "Blessed be this creature of Fire, in the names of Themis and Eunomia." Light the incense from the candle, and say: "Blessed be this creature of Air, in the names of Themis and Eunomia." Carry the incense and the candle around your home, wafting the smoke all around.

Say over the bell: "Blessed be this creature of Spirit, in the names of Themis and Eunomia." Carry the bell around your home, ringing it continuously.

Spell to Bring Peace Between Enemies/Rivals

Create a sacred space as detailed in Chapter One. Set up the altar as before. Take two small candles, scratch the name of one of the feuding parties onto one, and the name of the other onto the other. Put them at opposite sides of the altar.

Say: "Almighty Themis, daughter of Heaven and Earth, ruler of the cosmic balance, and your beloved daughter Eirene, as these candles burn away, may the enmity between (insert name) and (insert name) evaporate, and peace be left in its place."

After the candles have burnt for a while, move them a little closer together. Let them burn all the way down, every so often moving them closer, until they are next to each other, then take a piece of thread or cord and loosely bind them as one.

Themis's Lamp Spell

Aim: Lamp spell to bring light into hidden things, to help find lost things.
Tools: Photo or statue of Themis, lamp, tea light and holder, cedar incense.

Create a sacred space as detailed in Chapter One. Traditionally the lamp should be fuelled with sesame oil. Nowadays, however, it is not easy to obtain an oil lamp at all, in which case a lantern containing a tea light or candle may be used instead. The altar should be set up in the East, with the lamp at its centre.

MABON - AUTUMN EQUINOX

Statue of Themis on the roof of London's Old Bailey.

Say: "Almighty Themis, daughter of Heaven and Earth, ruler of the cosmic balance, to whom all things are known, by the symbolism of this lamp set in the East, where the lamps of Heaven, the Sun and the Moon, rise to illuminate the world, may I be enlightened with regard to …(detail what it is that you wish to understand and know more about.)"

Sit and meditate upon the question. If an answer is not immediately apparent, it may come to you in the next few days.

The Marjoram Dream Spell

Aim: For guidance through your dreams. The herb marjoram does not have a strong scent, so although it is here the active ingredient it is best mixed with other herbs, such as rosemary, sage or thyme. They should be burnt on a charcoal disc for three days in a row, ideally beginning at the dark of the Moon (when it is in the same position in the zodiac as the Sun), so that the third day will be when the crescent of the new Moon is first visible.

Each time, say: "Almighty Themis, daughter of Heaven and Earth, ruler of the cosmic balance, you who understand the secret workings of destiny, I ask for your guidance, that in the night, when deep sleep falls upon me, you may grant me a vision as to how I should proceed ahead with my life."

89

Put the ashes in an envelope, and place them under your pillow. The next night a dream should give you, the advice that you seek. The guidance may be literal or symbolic. Take note of every detail of your dreams that you can recall, no matter how small. It is best to keep a pen and paper by your bed, lest you forget it again afterwards.

Visualisation
By Seldiy Bate

Aim: If you are looking for guidance or the answer to a question, you may wish to formulate it in your mind before you begin. It's fine if you don't have anything specific, you will certainly get a message if you do this right! If you don't get very much through, don't worry, it isn't a sign of failure. Make notes and try again a day or so later.

Tools: A photo or statue of Themis, a smooth pebble or a tumbled crystal. It doesn't matter what gem you choose, although amazonite, green serpentine or agate all carry the right vibrations; it should be one that feels good in your hand. A grey candle and a holder. Melt the candle into the holder before use and make sure it's secure.

Incense: Frankincense, sandalwood or lavender.

Timing: Although this exercise works best at the Autumn Equinox, you can do it any time, especially if there's anything concerning you about justice, legal issues, or you have a need for harmony, balance and peace, reconciliation or agreement in some part of your life.

Before starting, relax, listen to some soothing music and have a bath, with a little fragranced oil in it if you wish. Create a sacred space as detailed in Chapter One. You can do this exercise sitting on a chair, with a table in front of you, or if you prefer to sit on the floor, have your items on a firm, low surface, like a draped box or a flat seat. The cloth should be a bluish green, or grey. Have the picture of Themis where you can see it. Light the incense and then light the candle and hold the stone in your hands. Feel its smoothness and weight, straighten your spine and feel the power of the stone travelling from your hands, down through your body and to your feet. Feel the connection with the earth, take some deep breaths and look at the room around you. Replace the stone and focus on the candle flame. Look at the picture of Themis and back to the candle flame. Close your eyes.

It is a mild Autumn afternoon and you are walking slowly on soft grass, looking down at your feet as you take steady steps forward. The air is fresh and fragrant and the light is different, as if you are in a new place. You stop walking and look up, and in front of you stands a magnificent Greek temple, with stone columns. It is identical to the one in the picture, but there is no one else there. You look around you and are aware of the sky, which is clear and a luminous greyish blue. There are no clouds and the light reflects off the stone of the temple.

As you watch, the Goddess Themis appears between two columns of the temple. She wears draped robes of blue-green and white, and her dark hair is swept up, showing her wide, wise forehead and her clear, all-understanding eyes. She holds a pair of scales and lifts them up, inviting you to use them and to take advantage of this time of true balance. Now imagine you are holding in your hands a thought, a problem, something that worries or hurts you, something that you wish to be rid of or at least to minimise. She moves forward and invites you to place it in one dish of her scales, you reach forward and do so, and as you do the scale dips down and the weight of this problem has been given to Themis. What will you do to bring harmony? What would you like to place in the other dish, to bring about balance, compromise, compensation? Tell her and put it in the other dish. The scales gradually return to equilibrium and she speaks to you now. If you wish to ask her a question, do it now.

Thank the Goddess Themis for her message and her words of wisdom. Her advice is impartial and her clear eyes see and know you; although Justice is blind, Themis sees all. Know that you must keep your actions just, keep true and keep your truth. She acknowledges you and turns towards her temple, carrying your problems to be reintegrated into the flow of the Universe. As she walks away, you too turn and walk for a while, feeling the soft grass beneath your feet. You realise you are walking towards a point of golden light and it gradually becomes focussed as a flame. It is the flame of the candle you have in front of you, you see it in your mind's eye. Open your eyes and there it is in front of you. Reach out and take your stone. Feel the smoothness and weight of the stone and let it connect you with the ground, look around you, see the room, hear the sounds around you, say something if you feel like it. Then stand up, return to your waking self and feel rejuvenated and enlightened. Make notes if you wish, put some music on and celebrate with a drink and a bite to eat. Take note of any dreams you have, they will be significant. Themis will be there whenever you need to put the balance back.

Autumn Equinox Spell to Bring Back Balance
by Seldiy Bate

Set up an altar, which can be a small table draped in a green or brown cloth. On it, put a vase of seasonal flowers, such as chrysanthemums, autumn foliage and sprigs of berries. If you have a figurine of the appropriate Goddess, such as Themis, Athena, or Venus place it on there too. A picture from the book is fine, or the Empress Tarot Card. A sheet of paper on which you have already drawn a vertical line to divide it into two sections. A pen with black ink, such as a fountain or felt-tipped pen. As you are going to write on the paper, have a backing board of some description, as you must do this as perfectly as possible. Have some Autumn Equinox incense ready, or a joss stick or oil burner. Appropriate perfumes are frankincense and myrrh (mixed) or sandalwood. A black candle on the left, a white candle on the right and nearby, a wax taper and matches.

At any time before you begin this spell, you should write out a rough version of what you intend to write. You are allowed up to six wishes.

On the left hand side, you will describe an issue that has been worrying you, a problem that you want solved, etc. Rough this out, think very carefully about how you express it. Opposite this "worry", write something positive which you feel balances it out, that can be the solution, or a hope and affirmation. For example, on the left hand column you might put "I am concerned about my financial situation", and in the right hand column "My work and money prospects will improve", or "I feel lonely", with "I am going to meet new people!" You can just focus on the one issue, or you may list up to six. Word it all carefully and spend time on the draft version, so that it is ready to be written out for real, on the actual date of the Autumn Equinox.

When you're ready to begin, make sure you won't be disturbed and put yourself into a relaxed frame of mind. Create a sacred space as detailed in Chapter One. Get your incense going and dim the lights. You may have a small light on, so you can see what you're doing. Now light your taper. Touch the black candle and send your intent into it, ask it to absorb that which is unwanted. Now light it, saying:

"This is the night, may it extinguish my fears!"

Touch the white candle, sending your intent into it, asking it to bring about your new requests. Light it, saying:

"This is the day, may it light up my hopes!"

Blow out the taper and put it to one side.

Stand in front of your altar, look at the two candles, burning side by side, and see this as the perfect balance between the two energies. Feel harmonised within yourself and say:

"Now that the night and the day are in balance, I seek to put balance into my life."

Now kneel at the altar or sit on the floor, with your notes, the paper, something to rest on and the pen. Write down your worry on the left, really feeling it, as you write it carefully in your best handwriting. Look at it for a few moments, then write its balancing request on the right, again, feel it and visualise it happening. Once you have finished writing, replace the paper on the altar. Everything else can be put aside. Stand up, look at the candles, then pick the paper up and turn it to face the two candles. Say:

"Goddess of the Equinox, I present my fears and my hopes.
Extinguish my fears, O Goddess of the Equinox!
Light up my hopes, O Goddess of the Equinox.
This is my request and, if it be right, May it come to pass!"

Fold the paper in half, down the middle, vertically, then continue to fold it up into a rectangle. Give thanks to your chosen Equinox Goddess, using her name, and in your own words, then extinguish the candles and put everything away.

Throw any draft notes away and put the folded paper under your pillow, paying attention to any dreams you have that night. Afterwards, you can put the paper away in a box, or under a weight. Look at it occasionally and when changes happen, put a tick or some notes near the appropriate phrase. Whenever anything negative is eliminated, cross it out.

After six months, dispose of the paper. You can burn it or put it in the recycling, it has done its work.

SAMHAIN
Cerridwen

Oh Great Goddess Cerridwen of the *cauldron*, I call to thee,
Stir your cauldron that your deep magic may *stir my soul*,
Bestow upon me the power o'herb and *moon*,
Fertility Goddess both mother and crone.
Inspirational Goddess, pure poetry divine,
Weaving words of spun gold
From that cauldron of thine.

Samhain (pronounce Sowen), is an Ancient Celtic fire festival held on October the 31st and was regarded as the end of the year. The Celtic people would slaughter their cattle at this time to provide food for the impending winter months. In modern times, it is also known as Halloween. It is believed that at this time, the veil between the worlds is at it thinnest, which means that it is a good time to try and communicate with loved ones that have passed over or simply to remember and honour the dead. It was once customary to put out food on the doorstep of your house for the wandering spirits. A semblance of this tradition survives today in the form of the 'Trick or Treat' custom at Halloween where children dress up and impersonate ghosts and expect to be given sweets to placate them. This time of year has always been associated with ghosts and the dead in many cultures across the world, from Mexico's Day of the Dead celebrations, to All Souls Day and Halloween.

Cerridwen, whose name means "White Sow", is the Welsh Goddess of Death and Rebirth as well as poetic inspiration. She is the Crone of Wisdom, the Keeper of the Cauldron. She is both a healer and a poisoner, a sorceress, a shapeshifter and one who knows the secrets of the Underworld.

Her legend is that she was the wife of a nobleman named Tegid Voel, and that they lived on an island in Llyn Tegid, also called Bala Lake, in the mountains of North Wales. They had two children, a beautiful daughter, Creirwy, light-skinned and radiant, and a son, Afagddu (also called Morfran), who was dark and ugly. Cerridwen sought to make this child wise, the most inspired amongst men, to compensate for his hideous appearance and to this end, she began to create a brew in her mystical cauldron. It was composed of charm bearing herbs that she gathered at the appropriate planetary hours, and spoke incantations over them. The first three drops of the magical potion would bestow wisdom, but the rest was a deadly poison. The mixture had to be simmered for a year and a day, and she left a young boy, Gwion Bach, in charge of stirring the cauldron. Now it happened by chance that towards the end of the year, as the boy stirred the boiling concoction, three drops splashed onto his thumb. His reaction was to stick his thumb in his mouth and from that moment, he gained knowledge of all things past, present, and future. And, since all of the rest of the contents of the cauldron were poisonous, it burst in two.

Gwion fled in fear, and Cerridwen, enraged at the loss of a year's toil, pursued him. Having gained magical abilities from the drops of wisdom, he changed himself into a hare and ran away. But she changed herself into a greyhound and gave chase. So he jumped into a river and became a fish, whereupon she followed in the form of a she-otter. Then he turned into a bird, but she chased him as a hawk. Finally he dropped into a heap of winnowed wheat in a barn, and turned himself into one of the grains. She then transformed herself into a black hen, scratched at the wheat until she found him, and ate him. He was in her belly for nine months, and then she gave birth to him. Because he was very beautiful, she could not bring herself to kill him, but instead she wrapped him in a leather bag, and cast him into the sea on the twenty-ninth of April. He was caught, near Aberystwyth, in the weir of Gwyddno, and found by Elphin who went there on May Eve expecting to find a large haul of fish, but instead found only this bag, which contained a miraculous child who could recite poetry at the age of one day. He named him Taliesin, meaning 'Radiant Brow'. Taliesin grew up to become a most renowned bard and poet.

As a matter of fact, Taliesin was a historical person, a court bard in sixth century Wales, some of whose poems have survived. This extraordinary story of his origin is a symbolic expression of the belief that poets derived their inspiration from the cauldron of Cerridwen. It also shows that they thought that, at least until recent times, this world and the other, magical world, could easily overlap.

Cerridwen is a lunar Goddess and seen both as mother and crone. She has powers of prophecy and can be called upon when you wish to gain insight or psychic power. As the stirrer of the cauldron, she can help with herbalism, healing, cooking or the making of potions. She can help you understand your inner self and your power animal, or to assist you to become a specific character when taking on a particular role; also to adapt to circumstances. As Goddess of Death and Rebirth, she can help you move on from a situation that has ended, allowing new energies to emerge. She is the patroness of bards, musicians, writers and poets, and is invoked to bring inspiration. Her animals are the greyhound, the otter, the hawk and the hen. She was also known as the Old White Sow. Her plants are trefoil, fern, vervain and wheat. Her colours are silver, dark blue, and black. Her symbols are the chalice and the cauldron.

Working with Cerridwen at Samhain can be beneficial for developing your psychic abilities, especially mediumship. It is also a idea good to consider the magical cauldron and work spells to aid the concoction of that which you wish to draw towards you in the coming year.

The Cauldron of Plenty

Aim: To be able to create a nourishing blend of good things in your life.

Tools: Large saucepan, red wine, muscovado sugar, cinnamon sticks, 2 oranges, 2 apples, nutmeg, cloves, a dash of marsala or sherry, brandy, cointreau.

Create a sacred space in the kitchen by cleansing the area with salt water as detailed in Chapter One. Place the red wine in the saucepan and add the apples. Stud the oranges with cloves and add them to the wine along with the cinnamon sticks and nutmeg. As you add each ingredient say: "I hereby add … (state something which you would like to bring into your life)."

Now add the dark muscovado sugar to taste, add quite a lot to sweeten the brew. Simmer over a gentle heat, stirring regularly. As you stir the potion, chant:

"Cerridwen, Cerridwen,
Stir my cauldron on this night.
Bring to me all I desire,
Blend my dreams upon this fire.
Cerridwen, Cerridwen,
Stir my cauldron on this night.
Cerridwen, Cerridwen,
Make it happen, make it right."

Do not allow the brew to boil as the alcohol will burn away. As you stir add a little of the marsala or sherry, a dash of the brandy and / or cointreau. Adjust to taste, always focussing upon your potion being a delicious blend of flavours and know that your desires will manifest as a perfect blend in your life. When the blend is just right, drink it, share it with friends and most of all, enjoy.

Visualisation

Aim: To heighten and develop your psychic abilities.
Tools: Photo or statue of Cerridwen, silver candle, candlestick, cedar or cypress oil. Cedar or sandalwood incense.

Create a sacred space as detailed in Chapter One. Light the incense and call upon the Goddess, say: "Great Goddess Cerridwen, Mother of the Moon, stir your cauldron for me this night. Crone of the midnight forest, guide me to your grove that I may share your secrets. Great Goddess Cerridwen, I bid you, hail and welcome!"

Take the silver candle and anoint it with the cedar or cypress oil. Focus upon the candle and ask that your psychic senses be heightened and detail which skills you wish to develop. Ask for what you wish to achieve.

Close your eyes and see yourself walking through a woodland scene at night. All around you the woodland is a deep midnight blue with silvery hues as the full moon shines down from the clear night sky above. You come upon a clearing in the woods and are drawn to a cauldron, steaming and bubbling over an open fire. As you approach the cauldron, you feel the warmth emanating from it as it bubbles and glows. Nearby, she emerges from the trees and you behold her for the first time, the Goddess Cerridwen, sweeping towards you in her long flowing robe, hair rustling in the breeze, partially covered by the hood of her long black cloak. She stops and greets you across the cauldron and as you gaze into her eyes, you see a steely strength, both mother and crone, the wisdom shining forth from her eyes as she asks you what it is that you seek. You tell her and she nods, before taking a pouch from within her cloak, she opens it to reveal a selection of herbs and roots. Cerridwen invites you to choose some, however many you like and you do so. Now, as you cast your wishes into the cauldron, cast also the herbs and roots that you have chosen. As each one enters the brew, say: "So mote it be!" When you have cast all of your herbs and intentions into the huge pot, Cerridwen starts to stir with her large wooden spoon. Round and round the mixture churns and she laughs, cackling with delight as the power of the cauldron builds. You laugh with her feeling the energy become stronger and stronger, delighting in the sense of her power, which starts to course through you as she stirs. You take hold of the wooden spoon and continue stirring as light pours forth from within the cauldron, illuminating the midnight grove. As the light shines brighter, you notice dark shapes that have appeared from the woodland around you both, they move towards you. As they venture out of the gloom, you see your ancestors, those that have gone before, come to meet you, to aid you in your task. They gather round and reflect the glowing light of the cauldron, no longer shades but beings of light. You continue stirring until the time feels right and then slowly stop, feeling enlivened by the experience and the joy that you have created as your wishes have been cast. Take some time with your ancestors, if you so wish. Cerridwen comes forward with her wooden spoon and uses it to serve you some of the brew from the cauldron. Taste it, so sweet and nourishing and as you drink it ensures the successful outcome of your wishes. Share the brew with your ancestors and know that they are happy for you, that they support you. When you feel ready, say your goodbyes to your ancestors and wish them well, for you shall meet again. Thank Cerridwen for her help and her blessings and take your leave of the midnight forest, safe in the knowledge that you can return again at any time. Walk through the woodland until you see a light ahead of you, walk into the light and through it and realise that it is the light of the candle flame burning atop your silver candle. See yourself sitting in front of your altar and bring your awareness back into your body. Wiggle your toes and in your own time, open your eyes. Let the candle burn all the way down.

"Is not my chair protected by the *cauldron of Cerridwen?*
Therefore, let my tongue be free
In the *sanctuary* of the praise of the Goddess."
~The Bard Taliesin

Hecate

Hail, many-named mother of the Gods,
Hail, mighty Hecate of the *Threshold*
Shape the course of my life with *luminous light*
and make it laden with good things.
Drive sickness and evil from my limbs.
and when my soul rages about worldy things.
Deliver me purified by your **soul-stirring rituals**.
Yes, give me your hand, I pray
and reveal to me the ***pathways of divine guidance*** that I long for,
then shall I gaze upon that ***precious light***
whence I can flee the evil of our dark origin.[i]

Throughout history there have been references to death at this time of year, and the Goddess Hecate is known as the Goddess of the Dead, of the Threshold between this world and the next. She is the Goddess of the Crossroads, or the meeting of three ways, and offerings would be left here in her honour. Hecate has always been associated with the creatures that dwell in the Underworld, the ghouls and the souls of the unquiet dead. Shakespeare acknowledged this in his play MacBeth by depicting the three witches casting their spells and summoning the Goddess Hecate. The words uttered by these witches have become famous as they circle their cauldron chanting: "Double, double, toil and trouble, fire burn and cauldron bubble!" In the film *Hecate Rising*, the

The witches from MacBeth summon the Dead in the film *Hecate Rising*

powerful magic of Shakespeare's three witches is re-enacted, as they circle the cauldron, reciting their spell, enthralling the audience, who are then invited to participate in their ritual to honour the Dead.

Hecate has permeated our cultures throughout the centuries and she is the Goddess who inspired the archetypal crone witch, an older woman with a black hat in front of a cauldron, with a black cat and a bat for company. The fact that these traditions have survived within our culture today is testament to Hecate's enduring power and popularity, if one can use that word to describe a Goddess with many darker attributes. She has never lost prominence, being adopted by one culture after another, constantly being re-invented and blended into new mythology.

Hecate became known as the Goddess of the Witches as sorcery and magic are also her domain, therefore she is an excellent Goddess to work with when casting spells or studying witchcraft. Ask her that your magic be good, powerful, effective and that your intentions be inspired.

Although she is often shown as a crone, an older woman, her triple aspect is sometimes seen as a representation of the three phases of womanhood, Maiden, Mother and Crone. This is a very popular concept in modern witchcraft, however the three phases of womanhood were not her original associations. Hecate has been adopted by many cultures for thousands of years and her attributes have evolved, so it is not surprising to find that this Goddess of many faces fulfils new roles in different ages.

Within Hecate's aspect as Goddess of the Dead, we also find her role as the Goddess of the Crossroads. At this time of Samhain we can ask her to help us to transform our lives, to grant our wishes and to help us to release that which we no longer want in our lives. Consider what you would like to release from your life, what you want to get rid of, and also what you would like to bring into your life in the coming year.

Hecate's third main aspect is that of Goddess of Madness, encompassing delusions and lunacy, yet at the same time she is the Goddess of Inspiration, including inner vision and psychic abilities. Ask Hecate for guidance and for the ability to be able to tell the difference between the two. For those who work as psychics and give readings, they would do well to ask Hecate for her blessing on their work, so that they may always know the difference between the voices of clairaudience and intuition and the voices of madness. Often when working closely with Hecate you may find yourself experiencing interesting situations which reflect her attributes. This can include complicated scenarios involving bereavement and grief, or dealing with people who are

suffering from mental illness. These are not to be feared, but instead see them as lessons, try to understand that which she is showing you. Working magically with Hecate at Samhain can be very powerful as we say goodbye to the old year and welcome in the new.

Burning Away The Old Spell

Aim: To release all that you want to be gone from your life.

Tools: Statue or picture of Hecate, black candle, candlestick, parchment, red ribbon or thread, small cauldron (or saucepan).

Incense: Sandalwood.

Prepare a sacred space as detailed in Chapter One. Light the incense and the black candle and call upon Hecate:

"I call upon you, great Goddess Hecate, Goddess of Sorcery and Magic, Goddess of the Witches. Be here at this time of Samhain and receive that which I wish to release from me."

Write on your parchment all that you wish to be gone from your life and read it aloud to Hecate, ask her to take it from you. Roll it up and tie it with red thread and light your parchment from the candle. Holding it safely above the cauldron or saucepan, say: "As this parchment burns, so do I burn away all that I wish to release from my life" (you can repeat the details if you wish). As the parchment burns, let it drop into the cauldron and watch it until it has all burned away and say: "So mote it be!"

Take note, if your parchment burns quickly and easily, then the spell will work swiftly without any hindrance. If the parchment takes time to burn or doesn't burn completely, then you may make encounter delays and obstacles. If this happens, re-light the parchment until it is all burnt. Thank the Goddess Hecate for receiving all that you wish to release and let the candle burn all the way down. Flush the ashes away in the toilet.

Mirror Spell - Can be Worked with Hecate or Cerridwen

Aim: To deflect negative energies from a person or persons that are making you feel uncomfortable.

Tools: Statue of Hecate or Cerridwen, black candle, candlestick, free standing mirror, pin.

Incense: Frankincense.

Oil: Banishing Oil.

RECIPE FOR BANISHING OIL

- ½ oz base carrier oil
- 5 drops juniper oil
- 5 drops clove oil
- 10 drops rosemary oil
- Obsidian or black onyx

Instructions
- Add the drops of oil with a dropper to the base oil and then add the crystal.
- Shake the oil until it is well blended.

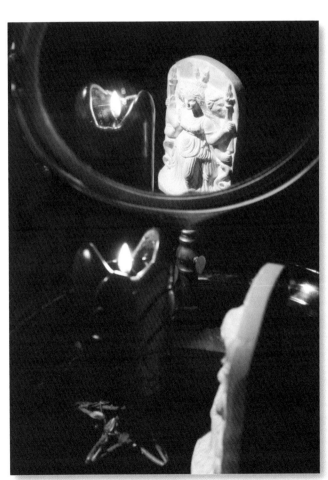

First prepare a sacred space as detailed in Chapter One. Light the incense and place it near the Goddess statue. Call upon the Goddess:

"I call upon you, Great Goddess Hecate/Cerridwen, Dark Goddess join me at this time of Samhain. Aid me in banishing all negative energies from around me and within me, to release that which no longer serves me."

Now using your pin, carve these words on the side of the candle, select which is appropriate: "I hereby release all that no longer serves me, from within me and without me. Let me be free from …(insert the details of what you would like to be free of)…"

Or, if it is a person that is upsetting you, write:

"You who cause me harm, I bind you that you may not hurt me on any level, in any form. May all the negativity and pain you have caused me be returned to you tenfold now. I take the anger and pain you have sent me and I send it back to you, right now! May it manifest in your life and bind you from causing me harm ever again. By the powers of Hecate / Cerridwen, So mote it be!"

Do not carve a person's name on the candle, even if you are sure that they have hurt you. Simply focus on the energy that you would wish to deflect away. Now focus on your candle and think about everything bad that you wish to release or everything bad that that person has done to you. Above all, be honest when pointing the finger of blame. Anoint the candle with banishing oil and place it in the candleholder. Set it up in front of the mirror and the Goddess statue and light it, so that the flame is reflected away from you. As the candle burns, chant:

"May harm return to sender,
May pain return to source,
To whomsoever has caused me harm,
May this spell take its course,
I bind you that you may not act,
Against me with your wicked pact,
May this spell in no way reverse,
Nor return upon me as a curse.
By the power of three times three,
Make it happen, so mote it be."

Repeat the verse three times. Leave the candle to burn down.

Visualisation

Aim: To reveal what is hidden, to discover a secret, to reveal something about oneself.
Tools: Statue or photo of Hecate, black candle, candlestick, sandalwood or cypress oil, sandalwood incense or make Hecate Incense.

Hecate Incense
■3 parts sandalwood
■1 part cypress
■Mix together and burn on a charcoal block.

Create a sacred space as detailed in Chapter One. Light the incense and place it by the photo or statue of Hecate. Call upon the Goddess and say:

"Great Goddess of the Underworld, I call to thee, join me at this time of Samhain. May your flaming torches shine brightly in the darkness, illuminating the shadowy world that evades me. Great Goddess Hecate, I bid you, hail and welcome!"

Take the black candle and anoint it with the oil. Focus on your intention and ask Hecate what it is that you seek, say:

110

"Great Goddess Hecate, I ask of you that at this time when the veil is at its thinnest, let me see that which is hidden. Let me see the truth in my situation (state what it is here). Open my eyes, Hecate, that I may see the truth with mine own eyes or that the answer be revealed to me in vision or dream. So mote it be!"

Light the candle and place it securely in the candlestick. Gaze into the candle flame and allow your eyes to lose their focus. Visualise the Dark Goddess beyond the flame, sitting looking through the flickering light towards you. Feel her presence and take note of any impressions that come to mind. Perhaps she speaks to you, or hands you a parchment with the answer written upon it. Perhaps you see images forming in the flickering candle flame or the answer to your question forms in your mind. This is the time when the psychic abilities of clairvoyance (clear seeing) and clairaudience (clear hearing) may become manifest. Feel the psychic impressions forming in your mind and take note of them. When you feel ready, re-focus your eyes and thank Hecate for her answer. Then bid her: 'Hail and farewell!' Let the candle burn all the way down.

The Mexican Day of the Dead in the film *Hecate Rising*

YULE
Holda

Hail Holda! *Luminous Lady* of Yule.
You cast a spell of sparkling snow,
your crystal flakes gently fall around us.
We call to you, star studded Goddess of winter climes,
and behold you *shimmering* in *frosted light.*
Shine upon us this dark December night and bring forth your *spark of light,*
that we may hold it within our hearts and welcome back the Sun.

Yule is the Anglo Saxon name given to the day of the Winter Solstice, the Midwinter Festival, which falls on either the 21st or the 22nd of December. This marks the shortest day of the year and the longest night. At this time, the darkest time of the year, it is customary to celebrate the sun, to call it back to warm the earth in the coming year.

Holda is the Teutonic Goddess of Winter. She is also known as the Germanic 'Frau Holle', made popular through Grimm's fairytales. She is connected with the hearth, the home, women and children. Holda is often represented as a beautiful young woman in white, or silver and white, and she sometimes has a blue veil. At other times, she can be represented as an old crone wandering through the world interacting with humankind. To the pure of heart and the hard working, she appears as a beautiful woman with long white hair. But to those who are unkind or lazy, she appears as a wizened old hag. Sometimes she is depicted as a woman with two faces; one young and beautiful, the other old and grim. She is the Goddess of Spinning, Childbirth and Domestic Animals, and is also associated with winter and witches.

Holda's myth tells how she would travel through the winter night sky in a sky chariot, drawn by wild woodland animals. She is accompanied by the souls of infants that had died

Our Yule Altar to call back the Sun

before they were named. Holda has no children of her own but is the protector of all children, she rocks the child's cradle when the nurse falls asleep, and is said to bring imaginative stories to children to help them sleep and dream. It is Holda who leads the souls of children that die to the Heavens, and when a child is born, it was believed that its soul entered the world through her magical and sacred pool. Pools, wells and fountains are sacred to Holda, and legend tells that she may appear as a white lady bathing in the water. Traditionally, young women who wished to become pregnant would bathe in Holda's icy mountain pool. She is associated with the sky, and also water, and it is Holda who was believed to create the snow, which falls at this time of year. As a Winter Goddess, she holds the promise of new life, so although her domain is that of the cold and the frost, she will make fields fertile again and she awakens the apple trees in the spring.

As Goddess of Wisewomen and Witches, she calls upon them to help dance the snow away. Her work is the explanation for many natural phenomena as snow is said to be made when Holda shakes her feather bed and fog is said to be the smoke from her fire. When it rains, it is believed to be Holda's washing day and thunder is said to be the rumble of her spinning wheel, and lightning is seen when she works at her flax. Her sacred symbols are the spinning wheel, water, ice, and snow, especially the snowflake.

Holda represents virtue and hard work and she rewards those who are industrious, bringing gifts to those who deserve it. She is the Goddess of Women's domestic chores and has sometimes been known to finish work for the diligent housewife, but also to undo the work of the housewife who is lazy. She is also the Goddess of Spinners and Weavers and is said to have taught women how to make linen from flax.

One of Holda's myths tells of a poor farmer whom Holda lured into her magical cave in the mountains. She appeared to him as a beautiful queen, surrounded by handmaidens, and led him to a cavern deep in the mountainside, which was filled with glittering gems and gold. She invited the farmer to choose a gift and instead of choosing the jewels, he chose the beautiful flowers of the flax plant that she held in her hand, a plant which he had never seen before. Holda gave him a bag of flax seeds, which he cultivated. She then taught the farmer's wife how to make linen cloth from the plants and the hard-working couple became rich through the blessings of the Goddess. Subsequently, Holda's sacred plant is the flax and her flowers are alpine flowers.

Holda can help us to bring about positive change in our lives by helping us to focus on what we need to do next. She inspires and encourages us to make that extra effort to complete anything which is unfinished in our lives as well as giving us that extra push to embark upon new projects. Ever since ancient times, she has always been known for helping and supporting us through the tough times and in today's world this is as important as ever. She is also strongly linked with a version of the rune Hagal, which is in the shape of a six pointed star, very similar to that of the snowflake. This is a very powerful rune, and if you meditate upon this symbol when focussing on your wishes and desires, it can help them to manifest more quickly.

Within the shape of the rune and the snowflake you can also find the star, and this connects us to another representation of the Winter Goddess, in the form of the fairy that we see on the top of the festive Christmas tree. She is the Fairy Godmother (or Goddessmother) to be found in many fairy tales who can wave her magic wand and grant your wishes. Her gentle energy blesses and nurtures us. She is beautiful and elegant and she shows us the way to work for the best in every situation.

At this time of Yule, it's traditional to feast, make merry and give gifts. Many Yule traditions involve bringing light into the home, such as lighting candles or burning a Yule log. The Yule log

116

was originally a large oak log which would burn for many days and was sacred the God of the Waxing Year. Burning the log is an act of sympathetic magic which encourages the actual heat and light of the Sun to return. The Yule Log cake is a remnant of this tradition and is shared in honour of the Winter Goddess and the God of Light. Evergreen trees are revered at this time, because their leaves do not wither or drop and they are considered to be magical providing a reminder that the plant life will continue through the dark months. It became customary to decorate an evergreen tree with ribbons and garlands and to hang lanterns on it. Then to honour the spirit within the tree, people would dance and sing around the tree and pour wine at its roots as an offering.

The Ancient Roman festivals of Saturnalia and Opalia took place in the days leading up to the Winter Solstice and were a time of rejoicing and feasting. The Goddess Ops would be honoured at this time, as she was the Goddess of Abundance and is depicted pouring out a never-ending supply of gifts for all the children from her Horn of Plenty.

Holda Spell

Aim: To bring inspiration and motivation to start or complete your work and projects.
Tools: Statue or photo of Holda, silver and blue candles (one for each wish), candlesticks, cinnamon oil, paper.
Timing: Winter Solstice night.

Prepare a sacred space as detailed in Chapter One. Call upon the Goddess Holda, say:

"Great Holda, Ice Queen, Goddess of Light, I call upon you to be present on this night. Bestow upon me your gifts so fair that I may be industrious in my work this year. Great Goddess Holda, I bid you, hail and welcome!"

Anoint a candle with cinnamon oil and focus upon it, asking Holda what it is that you wish for the coming year, which projects you need help and inspiration for and help to complete unfinished work or projects. Allocate one candle for each wish. As you finish one wish, light the candle and say: "So mote it be!" before moving onto the next candle. Repeat the process until all your wishes have been made. Take your piece of paper and draw the Hagal rune upon it. Close your eyes and meditate upon the rune, focus on its shape and repeat aloud what it is that you wish for. Still focussing on the Hagal rune, allow impressions and images to come into your mind. Open your eyes when you feel ready and thank Holda for bestowing her blessings upon you and then bid her: "Hail and farewell!" Let your candles burn all the way down.

Ice Queen Water

Collect some handfuls of the first snowfall of the winter. Save it in a glass bowl until it is melted. Add some holly leaves to the water and call upon the Goddess Holda to bless the water, say:

"Blessed Holda, beauty bright,
bestow your gifts on me this night,
that I may be fair of face, and enlivened with a gentle grace!"
Leave the water overnight and the following morning use it to wash your face.

Yule Sparkler Spell

When we make our wishes using sparklers, we are literally wishing upon a star, as the shape which is created by the sparkler resembles a star. Holding a sparkler whilst making your wish also reminds us of the powerful wands carried by every Fairy Godmother in every fairytale.

We create symbols in the air with our sparklers, especially protective magical symbols such as the pentacle. Light your sparkler and think about your wish, and as it burns, you can speak your wish out loud. If you are doing this with other people, you can all bring your sparklers together into a star shape. Send your thoughts out to the Goddess and ask for what you would like and she will bless you in the year ahead. End your ritual with the words: "So mote it be!" Share your cakes, a chalice of mulled wine with the group and offer some to the Goddess. As you finish your ritual remember to thank her for her gifts and her blessings.

Visualisation

Aim: To connect with the Goddess and to ask for guidance and motivation.
Tools: Photo or statue of Holda, silver candle, candlestick.

Create a sacred space as detailed in Chapter One. Light the silver candle and place it in the candlestick. Call upon the Goddess Holda and ask that she be present, say:
"I call to you, Holda, Lady of the Winter night, be here now and be my guiding light. At this time of winter dark, come forth that I might see the inspirational spark of light and motivation true, that I may complete my endeavours in honour of you. Great Goddess Holda, I bid you, hail and welcome!"

Close your eyes and visualise the candle flame flickering before you. See yourself walking in a snowy winter woodland scene, the snow crisp and bright beneath your feet, illuminated silvery blue by the light of the moon. Around you the trees appear magical, dusted with the frosty snowflakes. Ahead of you, you see a warm glow of fire upon the ground and as you approach the light, you enter a clearing in the woods. A figure kneels before the small fire, gently cultivating the flame so that it may flourish on this dark winter night. As you draw closer, the Goddess lifts her head and smiles at you, beckoning you to join her. You take your seat opposite her and the flame of Winter is between you. She is gentle and fair, wearing a pale blue veil about her head. When she smiles the warmth of the winter fire touches your heart. Sit with Holda for a while, talk with her, tell her of your wishes and intentions for the coming year especially in all matters pertaining to work. Listen to what advice she gives you. Perhaps she gives you a gift. When you feel ready, thank Holda for her presence and take your leave, safe in the knowledge that you can return here at any time. You walk back from whence you came, through the frozen woodland until you see a bright light shining ahead of you. Walk towards this light and enter its warm glow. As you walk through it become aware once more of the silver candle burning in front of your photo or statue of Holda, and bring your awareness back into your body. Wiggle your toes and in your own time, open your eyes.

Take note of all that Holda told you and any impressions that you have from the visualisation. Let the candles burn all the way down.

Bibliography

Chapter 2
(i) From *The Goddess Speaks* by Dee Poth, Sibyl Publications, 1998.
(ii) Manx Society Vol 16 Douglas: 1869.
(iii) Adapted from *The Gods Within* by Jean Williams and Zachary Cox, Moondust Books, 2008.
(iv) Adapted from the Orphic Hymn to Persephone.

Chapter 4
(i) from *Hedge Witch* by Rae Beth, Robert Hale, 1990.
(ii) This rite is adapted from the book *Hedge Witch* by Rae Beth, Robert Hale, 1990. Includes lines from Rae Beth's original text.
(iii) Adapted from Invocation to Flora by Morning Glory Zell.

Chapter 5
(i) and *(ii)* from *Under Regulus, a handbook for the magic of Sekhmet* by E. A. St. George, Spook Enterprises, 1995.
(iii) by Kai-Imakhu Senytmenu of the House of Netjer Kemetic Orthodox Temple.

Chapter 6
(i) Adapted from the Orphic Hymn to Gaia.
(ii) Adapted from *The Goddess Speaks* by Dee Poth, Sibly Publications, 1998.
(iii) Adapted from the Orphic Hymn to Ceres.

Chapter 7
(i) Orphic Hymn to Themis.

Chapter 8
(i) Hymn to Hekate and Janus by Proclus Diadochus (410-485AD), *Goddess Hekate* edited by Stephen Ronan, Chthonios Books, 1992.

About the Authors

Carrie Kirkpatrick is a television producer, photographer, presenter, TV psychic and author. She runs Divine Media (www.divinemedia.tv), producing television programmes about the esoteric world and historical mysteries and is a prolific photographer.

Carrie runs Goddess Enchantment workshops with her dear friend and colleague Kleo Fanthorpe, which have inspired the creation of these workbooks. Many of the images in these books were taken during the workshops, illustrating a visual and sensory celebration in honour of the Goddesses. For more information about Goddess Enchantment workshops and to view their online shop visit www.goddess-enchantment.tv .

Carrie is an ordained priestess of Hecate, Sekhmet, Erzulie and Papa Legba and specialises in teaching people how to connect with the Goddess energies. A regular guest and presenter on Sky TV and the BBC, Carrie is well known for her psychic readings and teaching. To find out more about Carrie and her work, visit: www.carrie-psychic.tv.

Gareth Medway is an historian and author, who specialises in comparative religion and the history of occultism. His book *Lure of the Sinister: The Unnatural History of Satanism* was published by New York University Press in 2001. Gareth is an ordained priest of the Goddess Themis.

Seldiy Bate is a musician and a mystic. She was initiated into Wicca many Moons ago and has taught and written about spellcraft and magick. She has spent many years researching the divine impulse behind folk customs and music and is inspired in everything she does, by the Muses, the many forms of the Goddess.

Now Available from Author Carrie Kirkpatrick

Goddess Enchantment, Magic and Spells takes you on a journey into the realms of magic and legend, as we retrace the myths of the Goddesses of old with a fresh perspective that makes them accessible in the 21st Century. Carrie Kirkpatrick opens the doorway to the magical realms of the Goddesses, inviting you to partake in visualizations, spells and magical rituals designed to help you fulfill your potential. See the Goddesses come to life in vibrant and magical photographs, connect to them and gain from their inspirational blessings. *Goddesses Love, Abundance and Transformation* introduces the Goddesses that can help you to transform your life and manifest the love and abundance that you desire. Visit www.gravedistractions.com for more information about this title.

Volume 2:
Goddesses of Love, Abundance, and Transformation

Goddess Enchantment

Magic & Spells

Written & Photographed by
Carrie Kirkpatrick

Coming Soon: *Tarot Cards At Dawn*

Divina Lovett has a new job. She is to appear on television demonstrating her skills as a tarot card reader and psychic. Nervously, she turns up for her first day at the psychic channel and finds herself immersed in a world of low budget interactive television and adult sex chat lines. The situations she encounters range from the ridiculous to the bizarre, the inspirational to the downright funny, as she proceeds on her own spiritual journey, as represented by the Major Arcana in the Tarot deck. Divina Lovett is the Bridget Jones of the psychic world adrift in a sea of low budget TV and adult entertainment. *Tarot Cards At Dawn* is a fictional story based on Carrie Kirkpatrick's years spent in front of the camera as a celebrated TV psychic on the UK's psychic television channels. Visit www.tarotcardsatdawn.com for more information about this book.

CPSIA information can be obtained
at www.ICGtesting.com
2371LVUK00002B